Just Believe

Commonsense Spirituality for the 21st Century

Lisa Tarves

Copyright © 2015 Lisa Tarves

All rights reserved. No part of this book may be used or reproduced by any means, graphic, electronic, or mechanical, including photocopying, recording, taping or by any information storage retrieval system without the written permission of the publisher or author except in the case of brief quotations embodied in critical articles and reviews.

ISBN: 978-0-9966531-0-7

ISBN-10: 0996653104

Library of Congress Control Number: 2015912195

Writestream Publishing books may be ordered through booksellers.

Because of the dynamic nature of the Internet, any web addresses or links contained in this book may have changed since publication and may no longer be valid. The views expressed in this work are solely those of the author and do not necessarily reflect the views of the publisher, and the publisher hereby disclaims any responsibility for them.

The author of this book does not dispense medical advice or prescribe the use of any technique as a form of treatment for physical, emotional, or medical problems without the advice of a physician, either directly or indirectly. The intent of the author is only to offer information of a general nature to help you in your quest for emotional and spiritual well- being. In the event you use any of the information in this book for yourself, which is your constitutional right, the author, and the publisher assume no responsibility for your actions.

Printed in the United States of America.

Writestream Publishing, LLC
Parker Ford, PA
www.writestreampublishing.com

Believe in Love

Believe in Magic

Believe in Angels

Believe in Miracles

Believe You Can Achieve Anything

Believe You Are Fearless

Believe That Everything Happens For a Reason

Believe That Anything Is Possible

Believe That Your Thoughts Can Heal Your Body

Believe in Fairies

Believe in the Unbelievable

Just Believe

Dedications

First, to my parents Craig and Patricia Brown for your unconditional love throughout my life. You accomplished what wonderful parents do by giving me the security that comes with sturdy roots and the freedom that accompanies spirited wings. I miss you every day. We ARE connected. I will see you again.

To my husband Scott for your love, patience and never-ending support. Your gifts to me have been endless. I'm grateful every day for your confidence in me and your ability to stay on the rollercoaster ride that is our life together. You inspire me to be better. I love you.

To my children Nicholas, Kristyn and Lauren for making my job as a mom so easy. Nicholas, you have the biggest heart and kindest soul of anyone I know, and you've become an incredible man. Kristyn, you are incredibly beautiful, strong, fearless and independent; I am truly in awe of you. Lauren, you have many gifts that come with a caring heart and a thoughtful nature; your future has endless possibilities. I am proud of each of you, and I love every moment of being your mom.

To my brother Greg Brown for helping me remember things I'd forgotten, for making me laugh, and for always having my back.

To my mother-in-law Margaret Baughman for making sure I keep walking my talk and for always being encouraging.

To Shirley Bowers-Brown for being an extraordinary wife to my father for too short a time. You made him happy again and for that I am grateful. Thank you for caring for, and honoring him while he lived and as he died.

To my friend and business partner Daria Anne DiGiovanni for your contagious creative spark and captivating inspiration.

Without each of you, my life would be so much less. I love you all!

Foreword

I met Lisa Tarves via a Google search in December of 2012. A longtime resident of Florida, I was visiting family in the suburban Philadelphia area and thought it would be fun to have a consultation with a metaphysician. I was looking for someone who could help guide me through the personal challenges confronting me at the time.

Lisa's website popped up first after I typed in the search parameters. When I saw her picture, I immediately sensed she was a competent, compassionate, and knowledgeable professional. And while all of those things turned out to be true, I still had no idea that I was about to embark on a life-changing relationship. A relationship that would offer not only genuine friendship but also an opportunity to join forces to realize my professional goals of starting a successful internet radio network and becoming a publisher.

After reading about her services, I contacted Lisa immediately to set up a session, which exceeded my expectations. During that call, she went above and beyond to answer my questions fully, with no concern about running over our allotted time. Our friendship and business partnership developed quickly from there.

Having listened to Lisa as a guest on several internet radio programs, she was my first choice to host a metaphysical show when I conceived of the Writestream Radio Network in early 2013. Not only did she demonstrate remarkable intuitive ability but she also exuded striking authenticity and genuine compassion for her guests and callers. I knew she was the perfect person to talk spirituality and figured this would also provide a vehicle for her to promote her wonderful book, *Just Believe*. When I called her to pitch the idea, I was delighted by her exuberance and enthusiasm. From that point on, Lisa became my partner in this venture, which at first was intended to support my marketing efforts on behalf of clients whose books I either edited or ghostwrote. Once again, I had yet to see the full picture.

Turned out, Lisa was a force of nature – an accomplished woman with an impressive resume including three successful businesses and corporate marketing experience in the telecommunications industry aside from a remarkable talent for writing and editing.

In my review of the first edition of *Just Believe*, I wrote, "Part autobiography and part Spirituality 101. Lisa first introduces herself to her readers, sharing in down-to-earth, 'real' language her experience as a young child with a remarkable sense of the unseen world including the ability to see and communicate telepathically with angels. Having established herself as a legitimate source of information on the topic, Lisa then delves into various aspects of spirituality with humor and authenticity."

In the two-and-a-half years of Writestream Radio Network's existence, *Just Believe with Lisa Tarves* has consistently drawn the biggest audience amid a seven-day line-up of excellent hosts and programs. Judging from the numbers, it is obvious that Lisa's charm, personality, and skill are recognized and appreciated by listeners all over the world.

On a personal level, she has been one of my most passionate champions and coaches, always ready to offer advice as to how to best proceed with a project or promote my work.

Somewhere along the way, Lisa and I conceived of Writestream Publishing and after much deliberation and planning, officially launched the company in June of 2015. Despite my own wordsmithing skills, it's impossible for me to express the full extent of my gratitude and excitement to her for everything she's done to make this dream a reality. I am so proud to be Lisa's friend and business partner and look forward to our mutual success.

I have no doubt you will enjoy and benefit from the sage advice and spiritual knowledge Lisa shares within these pages. When you finish, please consider writing a review to let others know about this excellent book.

Thank you, Lisa, for your presence in my life. The best is yet to come!

Daria Anne DiGiovanni

www.dariadigiovanni.com

Preface

In September of 2012, the first edition of *Just Believe* was published. Much has occurred in my life since then, some magnificent and some tragic. Around February of 2015, I began considering republishing *Just Believe* as a second edition. I was never thrilled with the cover, the lack of a subtitle, and a few other issues caused by the lack of guidance through my then, publisher. I really craved a new cover that reflected my personality and style, a subtitle that clearly explained what the readers would find in the book, and I wanted to add updates on some of the things that have occurred since the first edition. Although much of the book is as it was in the first edition, there are many updates and additions, but the chapters and general ideas are the same.

In August of 2014, my father was diagnosed with pancreatic cancer. It was terminal. My dad was my "spiritual buddy". We shared the same beliefs on metaphysics and spirituality and had hundreds of lengthy conversations on the subject. Many of my family members on his side have psychic gifts I talk about in this book. My dad, my mom, and my grandmother are often mentioned within these pages. My mom had very unexpectedly passed away a few days after knee replacement surgery in April of 2008 which I talk about in Chapter 11.

My dad fought bravely to survive and hold on as long as he could, but in doing so he suffered. As too many of us know, cancer is a horrible disease. Pancreatic cancer is many times immediately diagnosed as terminal. I watched this disease take a strong, healthy, happy man and quickly and painfully destroy him. He made it to his milestone 80th birthday on Christmas Day, although I'm fairly sure he didn't know what day it was by that point. He passed away on January 5th. Then, in February my grandmother died at 100 years old, just eight weeks after losing her eldest son.

These losses have no doubt altered my life. Losing one's parents is something most of us must experience during our lifetime but it is still incredibly heart-wrenching. The importance of my telling you this story in the preface to the second edition of Just Believe is that in my grief and my asking the question we all ask, "WHY?", I suddenly had to consider if I still believed what I had written in 2012. Could I still honestly feel pride in the words I'd put to paper three years earlier? Did I still myself *believe*? Did this book still represent my personal truth? I will admit I wasn't sure. I hurt. I grieved. I questioned why such painful deaths for my mom, my dad, and my grandmother. Why the suffering?

I think many people come to a point in their lives where they have a crisis of faith. Why would I be the exception? The answer was simple. I thought since I had been talking to deceased people for my clients for as long as I can remember, I would have plenty of interaction with my family members after their passings. I had been seeing angels since I was a little girl. I had been comforting people in mourning with messages from their loved ones for years. And, where were my parents? My grandmother? I was getting NOTHING! I began feeling a bit of resentful for my work and started reconsidering everything I was doing in my life. I had spent the last several years helping people heal their pain. Did I not matter? Was I not worthy of contact with spirits of the people I missed so much? I just didn't get it. And honestly, parts of it I still don't understand.

I spent many months reading my book over and over, carefully contemplating the words I had written three years before. It took time and a lot of real soul searching, but I can now finally say that I have my answers. I don't understand why, but I cannot communicate with my parents or my grandmother or any of the people I've lost like I can for other people. It's just not what God wants for me right now. I get a small sign here and there – something out of the ordinary that I can attribute to one of them. But, that's about it, and I just had to accept it. And, most days I do. Some, eh, maybe I don't feel quite as much acceptance.

Most importantly I can finally say what I wrote in this book originally; the beliefs I have, the memories I shared and the "just knowing" I am so grateful for, are still there. The grace God has shown me in a million ways throughout my life still keeps on coming, and I am thankful. I am blessed. I honestly do still believe.

Many wonderful things have happened since the first edition of Just Believe as well. My friend and business partner, Daria Anne DiGiovanni and I grew our radio network, Writestream Radio, which airs my weekly radio show, (Go on and guess what it's called...YEP, *Just Believe!*) into a seven-day-a-week lineup of incredible programs with gifted hosts and inspiring and talented guests. Most recently, Daria and I launched Writestream Publishing, LLC where we help individuals with the dream of having their story in print achieve that goal and get their book published. We are truly moved by our clients and their work. We take a very personal approach with each of our authors allowing us to get to know them personally and work very closely with them through the publishing process. I can comfortably speak for both of us when I say we each feel gratitude every single day for the amazing group of talented writers and overall inspirational people we meet through this work.

If you bought this book a second time, I hope you pick up on the updates and changes. If you're reading it for the first time, I hope you enjoy it, learn from it and most importantly, find inspiration in the words.

Thank you for choosing to read *"Just Believe: Commonsense Spirituality for the 21st Century."*

With Love,

Lisa Tarves

Table of Contents

CHAPTER 1	Introducing...ME!	1
CHAPTER 2	A Day in the Life of a Lightworker	9
CHAPTER 3	Why I Believe What I Believe	19
CHAPTER 4	What Is a Lightworker and Are You One?	29
CHAPTER 5	What the Heck is a Chakra?	37
CHAPTER 6	Living as an Empath	47
CHAPTER 7	Judgment Sucks!	55
CHAPTER 8	Forgiveness	67
CHAPTER 9	Energy Vampires	75
CHAPTER 10	Happiness Is Simply a Choice	85
CHAPTER 11	Angels and Spirit Guides	91
CHAPTER 12	Everything is Energy and Energy Can Heal	103
CHAPTER 13	The Scoop on the Law of Attraction	111
CHAPTER 14	Those Pesky Little Etheric Cords	119
CHAPTER 15	There is No Death	125
CHAPTER 16	Why Not Just Believe	137

"Knowing others is wisdom, knowing yourself is enlightenment" – Lao Tzu

Chapter 1

Introducing... Me!

This book might be a bit surprising to many of the people who know me personally. Friends and relatives who know me as this "semi-normal" woman (never completely normal because that would be boring, and I am firmly against being boring), with a good sense of humor, who enjoys a great dive bar, loves planning parties, is fiercely independent, avoids drama at all cost, is as stubborn as they come and as loyal as a dog. I love country music, classic rock, and even classical pieces. I never back down from a fight when sticking up for what's right and for the people I love. I have often been heard saying when defending my children, "Don't you mess with my babies"! Even though they are currently 22, 21 and 17, they are still and forever will be my babies.

I'm not a fan of mornings, but I enjoy staying up late into the night. I love a cold beer, a glass of wine or two and even some tequila shots when there's something to celebrate (and that's not hard to find). That's the person my friends and family know. So if they happen to read this book, most of them will be learning about an entirely new side of me that they had no idea existed.

I've kept many secrets about myself and my life that I've just begun revealing over the last few years. I have a couple of special gifts, and that's what I talk about throughout this book. So why did I keep these gifts a secret? The truth is for a long time I didn't even know that I possessed special gifts. I was who I was, and I just assumed everyone experienced something similar. When

I did finally realize I knew some things most people didn't, I was just too busy living my life. I was raising young children, working full-time, managing my home and the typical things we all do day to day. I had a very busy and hectic, but happy life. Every once in a while I would have a few moments when I was able to contemplate how or why I was "different", but I had no room in my life to make this a priority. So many years went by before began to share my story.

Others reading this might be equally surprised that someone with my gifts and beliefs isn't a more conventional spiritual teacher with a more serious, mystical, regimented lifestyle. They might think a person who does the type of work I do and has intuitive abilities can't possibly live the normal life that I have so far and will continue to describe to you throughout this book. Believe me when I say I have *definitely* had some incredible experiences. But after years of not making a big deal out of the unusual things I knew and years of being an average down-to-Earth person, I have learned how to live normally. Whatever "normal" might happen to be.

I've written this book in a language and style that expresses my personality. The way I talk, write and communicate with people day-to-day. It's me. Like it or not, it's not fake or made up, and it's not ghostwritten by someone with more writing experience. I've written every word and what you'll find in these pages is about my life so far. This book explains my gifts and gives my perspective on topics that are spiritual and metaphysical in nature.

I've wanted to write a book for many years. Writing has always been a great love of mine. I've always kept a diary or journal and enjoyed writing papers and articles. When I was in fourth grade, I was tasked with writing a book for English class in school. I remember very little about the book itself, but I do recall making the book cover out of left-over wallpaper that I found in the basement that was hanging on our kitchen walls. That book, which I've long since lost and forgotten the title or even the subject, was chosen to be read over the loudspeakers at our local mall and displayed along with other books from children in other grades. My parents were of course very proud. I specifically remember my grandfather saying to me, "Lisa, you should keep writing. This could be just the start for you."

I'm a Gemini. One of the traits that come with being a classic Gemini that has helped me over the years is that I've always been a good communicator. As many Gemini's do, I love being the center of attention. Put me in a room full of people all eyes on me listening to what I have to say; no, I'm not intimidated or afraid. I absolutely love it! Crazy right? I don't fear public speaking, and I don't fear death; these are said to be the top two fears of humans. Interestingly enough most fear public speaking first and then death in that order. But those fears just aren't on my list. Now, spiders, bats, frogs and snakes, well that's another story!

I am a Metaphysician by education. I earned my Master's Degree in Metaphysical Science and Board Certification as an expert in the field of Holistic Health. I'm a natural born healer and intuitive. I am also a Usui and Tibetan Reiki Master. What do all those titles mean? What do I do? I help to heal people using various energy modalities. I intuitively counsel and guide individuals with the assistance of angels and spirit guides. I read people. I help my clients save themselves from their worst enemy; usually the very face staring back at them in the mirror. I help them find a comfortable and secure balance in their lives. I try my best when given the opportunity, to make my clients feel passionate about life again. To help them realize, they have no cap, no ceiling on what they can become or accomplish in their lives. I assist my clients in correcting negative thought patterns and turning them into positive thought patterns. It's why I believe I was chosen to be a lightworker on our planet in this lifetime, NOW.

When you read the following pages, you may think someone with my intuitiveness would have a piece-of-cake sort of life. How could I possibly mess anything up in my personal life when I know the things I know and have an almost direct line to the angels? (You'll read about that in Chapter 3.) Well, trust me when I tell you I've made a lot of mistakes in my life. I'll give you some details on just some of them in later chapters. But, did I know I was making each mistake at the time? In most situations, yes, I felt it in my gut. But just like anyone else, I didn't necessarily want to listen to that voice inside me. That voice that lives in that place inside us where we feel a strange, nagging sensation when we are faced with a tough decision or when our conscience is calling us out. We sometimes know the right thing to do but still resist or ignore it. I wanted to get my way and have whatever it was I desired. So, just like everyone else with a conscience, I wrestle, even still, with mine too. But, it's a little bit different for me. The simplest way I can describe what that sensation in my gut feels like for me would be to say it's kind of "supersized". It is the strong intuitive sense I was born with and have lived with since. It can be so intense it will leave me physically sick or cause extreme anxiety if I ignore it. However, my stubborn side has on more than one occasion won the struggle with my intuition, and I've put myself in a position to get kicked in the head by reality. My desire for certain things has affected my judgment many times. I've wanted to trust people who didn't deserve my trust. I've often expected that since I'm a good and honest person who always tries to do the right thing that everyone will do the same. This sadly as we all eventually learn, isn't the case. I've struggled with the things most people struggle with. Things have been hard at times for me just like for everyone else. I've been hurt, and I've made poor choices. And hindsight is....well just that, hindsight.

  What I've now learned to do differently is what led me down the spiritual, metaphysical and holistic path to teach, guide and heal others. What I've learned is to work hard each and every day to make sure that no matter what happens to me and around me, I always stay strong and as positive as possible. Most importantly, I always keep things in perspective. It is rarely easy and is certainly not always immediate. There are times when I don't handle stressful situations in my own life the way I teach others to manage them. I'm not hypocritical; I'm human. I've had my fair share of flip-outs and meltdowns. When I get hurt, I often take a little time to lick my wounds before forgiving. Once I've forgiven, I don't necessarily put myself back in the same situation again or allow the same person that caused me pain, anxiety or stress back into my life. I don't spend time around people that somehow always manage to make me think less of myself. I put distance between myself and situations like these.

  Throughout it all, the good and the bad, I insist on keeping my life in perspective. I thank God daily for the blessings I have in my life right now at this very moment. The health of my children, my relationship with my husband, my love for my work, the friends in my life and so much more! I appreciate everything I have and everyone I love and who loves me. Sometimes I'm forced to search long and hard to find the positive side at the end of the day. With the work I do, I see and hear about outrageous dramas and unimaginable traumas every day. It's heart-breaking to see people in so much pain, and I fight to pull one positive out of any situation. And drama comes knocking on my door sometimes on my door sometimes even though I try desperately to keep it out. So, I find a way to hold on, be strong and make the very best out of everything that happens. Even when it seems like there is nothing good to find in a situation, I will eventually find something somewhere.

What you will be reading on the following pages is more than 40 years in the making. It is an eclectic and diverse collection of topics that are each of great significance in my life. These are some of my most passionate of passions. Sometimes while you're reading this book, it will seem I am writing an autobiography about growing up as an intuitive and healer and about my personal life. Other times it might feel more like a textbook. Either way there is a lot to learn. Whether you're interested in spiritual and metaphysical topics purely for educational reasons, or you're looking to read about what it's like to be able to see angels and know about an afterlife that is as real as the life you are living now, I will be talking about all of it and mixing it up just a bit, so you don't get bored.

I hope you enjoy what I *believe* to be my first of many books.

"You were given this life because you are strong enough to live it." ~ Unknown

Chapter 2

A Day in the Life of a Lightworker

It's a beautiful sunny day in early April. The weather is much warmer than what is typical for this early in the spring. I'm sitting in my office with a new client named Angela. My office is a safe, healing space where people always remark on its comfortable energy. Next to my desk is a large bookshelf full of metaphysical topics ranging from the Bible and the Tao to spell casting and fairy magic. Hanging on the wall across from my desk is a large ornate gold cross. A Buddha statue carved from wood sits on a table that I call my altar directly beneath the cross. On each side of my altar on the floor sit tall bamboo plants. All throughout the room that has dark gold painted walls I'm surrounded by stunning crystals I've collected over many years. Each crystal has its own metaphysical, healing, and spiritual properties. Each in its own way brings me great joy and peace. My office often called a meditation room, feels and is a protected, sacred, healing space.

Angela and I had met less than five minutes before. She's a beautiful young woman in her early twenties. I intuitively acknowledge that her inner beauty radiates from her as clearly as her outer beauty shines to the rest of the world. However, as I look at Angela, I can sense an underlying pain that I believe she has carried with her for many years. After just a few moments of making her comfortable by exchanging pleasant and light- hearted conversation, I ask her what brings her to me. She takes a deep breath looks down at her hands and her eyes well up with tears. I ask her then where her pain is coming from, and she sadly acknowledges that she really doesn't know. She struggles through her tears and says, "I just feel lost and without a purpose right now. Something feels off inside me. It's like I'm missing something I'm supposed to do or supposed to know that should be so obvious because it's right in front of me, but I can't tell what it is. I'm sad and depressed which isn't normally how I am. I feel like I'm wasting a significant time in my life by not enjoying it when I should be happy. I feel alone even when I'm with my family, friends and my boyfriend who are all great people that I truly love.

I immediately feel compassion for Angela. I understand her situation well. She is one of the many clients who express this same emotion to me, day after day sitting in the same chair as she is now. She goes on to tell me she has tried to bring herself out of this funk for many months. She is even on an antidepressant medication prescribed by her doctor who diagnosed that she has a mild case of clinical depression. She tells me she doesn't think the medication is making a difference. She says it's been several weeks since she began taking the drug, and she isn't feeling any better. Feeling great sympathy for her situation, I explain to her that I am intuitively sensing an energy block within her.

It feels to me like a blockage that has been building for many years which until recently she's been successfully able to suppress. People can suppress their pain for a period of time, but it's unhealthy to do so. Eventually, pain must be healed. The energy blockage has become so intense that she is overwhelmed with negative emotions. The negative emotion has created her depression. I tell her that one or maybe more than one of her energy centers called "chakras" looks to be blocked. I describe to her the way energy flows throughout our bodies. If negative energy gets stuck in one of our primary energy centers (chakras), it will dramatically affect our quality of life.

Although Angela looks a bit confused, she tells me she is interested in learning more. She begins asking what in the world a "chakra" is and follows that with other questions about these energy centers. I give her a brief lesson on the seven major chakras that make up the human energy field. If there is negativity or damage in the energy field, it can be seen in a person's aura, which is a word with which she is more familiar. She then asks the next logical and commonly asked question, "Can you fix it?" I tell her that I can absolutely remove the blockage, however, there are two parts to healing the energy center problem for good.

    First I explain to her that I will use an energy healing method called Reiki to cleanse and heal her chakras. I go on to explain that we must, however, take it a step further. We need to figure out what caused the damage in the first place. She looks a bit confused and even a little afraid at this point. This fearful look is one I have seen before on the face of a client. Many of my clients come to me expecting a magical healing that requires no follow-up, no work and no change on their part. Change is rarely comfortable or easy for anyone. So at this point in our conversation I begin my routine lecture on how the mind, body, and spirit work together to create our emotional and physical health. Healing the existing physical blockage is just one step. In order to keep her energy flowing freely throughout her body permanently, more work must be done. We must get to the root cause of the energy block; the root cause of her unhealed pain.

    I ask Angela to lie down on my Reiki table while I scan her body for energy blockages or muddied chakras. I explain that the process of Reiki is like an "air massage". She will more than likely feel energy coming from my hands and going into her body even though I am not physically touching her. I ask her to take a couple of cleansing breaths and to close her eyes, relax, and to allow whatever happens to happen within her without fear. I calm her nervousness by explaining that what she will be experiencing is energy that is coming directly from the universe, directly from Spirit, directly from God. This energy is love and only pure love.

    Using an ability that I can only describe as an intuitive gift I was born with, I use my hands to hover an inch or two over her physical body. I am then able to look within and carefully examine and study each of the chakras. When I'm doing a scan, I'm checking the color of each chakra to make sure they are bright and clean. I check their size; they should not be over or undersized. I finally check their speed to make sure they are spinning as they should.

    As I usually do with my clients, I begin Angela's scan with the root chakra also known as the first chakra. Immediately I sense this chakra is completely blocked. Suddenly, the name "Jack" comes to me. I keep that information to myself for now. I continue to scan her sacral, solar plexus, and heart chakras. When I reach her heart chakra, I hear the name "Jack" again, and I make a mental note to ask her about this after the healing part of our session is complete. I continue by scanning her throat, third eye, and crown chakras.

After the scan is complete, I go back to where I started at her root chakra where I initially felt a total lack of energy flowing during the scan. I begin the process of clearing and opening this chakra feeling the powerful, loving and pure energy pouring out of my hands into her body. After several minutes, the root chakra begins to become a brighter and brighter red and the muddiness starts to dissipate. Then slowly like watching a flower bud bloom I see the root chakra open. Feeling and intuitively seeing this happen with a client always feels so good to me that I can't keep from smiling. I'm confident that I've done good work. I continue the healing looking next at her sacral chakra, and I'm not surprised to notice it is a little brighter orange than it appeared during the scan. The new energy flow from the first (root) chakra has instantly allowed energy to begin flowing to the chakras above it. I move to her solar plexus that is now a brighter yellow, and I clear out any muddiness that remains. Moving to her heart chakra after only a few moments of energy work, it becomes the beautiful green it should be. I examine her throat chakra next, and it responds by becoming bright blue. Subsequently, I move on to her third eye where I see a lovely shade of indigo. I finish with her crown chakra that becomes a beautiful shade of violet. I scan the chakras one by one again to make sure they are all spinning at the correct speed and that they are each the appropriate color and size. I allow her to lie still while she takes in the peacefulness that has come over her.

Angela is in a very relaxed state right now, so I want to give her a few moments to lie on the table and slowly become alert and aware of her surroundings. Then I very softly tell her that only when she is ready she can slowly sit up. Shortly after that she opens her eyes and looks at me with a beautiful and peaceful look that even if I live to be 120 years old I will never get tired of seeing after a healing session. Angela just says, "Wow!" as she slowly sits up.

As she's enjoying the calm and intense feeling of being healed and renewed, I explain that we still have a little bit of work to do. After she settles back into the chair across from my desk, I gently ask her about the name Jack. Her eyes get large, and her jaw drops a bit. She looks at me with amazement and then says, "Jack was my father."

Angela explains that her father passed away when she was 16 years old. He had been a heavy drinker and physically abusive to her mother, her siblings and herself. She had always wanted and worked hard for his approval. She just wanted him to love and be proud of her. Despite her effort, no matter how well she did in school, no matter how hard she helped with chores around the house, no matter how talented she was at playing the piano, she never seemed to get the approval she desperately longed for from her father. To me, this explains everything. I understand now that her root chakra blockage is the result of her childhood, and it is also the cause of her recent unhappiness. My job now is to make her understand how her past has created her emotional, physical and spiritual present. I explain to her that to keep her chakras balanced and for her to continue on her path of renewed physical, emotional, and spiritual health, we must address the issue with her father.

I begin by asking her some specifics about her childhood. And discover that she has never permitted herself to forgive her father for his abuse or even her mother for not protecting her and her siblings by leaving the situation. She tells me that although she will always love her father, and there is a part of her that misses him, she cannot forgive the pain he inflicted on her and her family. She says she does not feel he deserves her forgiveness.

So here it is laid out before us; the "root" cause of her pain and suffering. At this point, I say to her, "Angela, you do need to forgive your father for you to maintain a healthy body and mind." She stares at me stubbornly as I continue, "You do not forgive him for his sake. Forgiveness is purely for you; for your present and future health and happiness." I explain to her that by forgiving him she is not condoning his behavior or making excuses for the pain that he caused. She is merely saying that she will not allow him to hurt her anymore. She is just saying that she will not allow him to hurt her anymore. She is releasing him and letting go of her pain and her anger. Even though her father is no longer alive, by not forgiving him she is still giving him power over her life. She cannot allow the way he chose to live his life to in turn, affect her life negatively and continue to cause her pain. It must end. She must decide that she will not allow herself to be affected by the past to the point that her future is destroyed because of her parents' mistakes even for one more day. To heal, she has to begin the process of forgiving.

Angela and I worked for several weeks on how to forgive her parents.

Although it was not an instant transformation or the magic she may have been hoping for, I am pleased to say that today she is happy and healthy. She is no longer taking prescription medication (after consulting with her medical doctor who agreed she could begin the process of weaning off the drug). Her heart is now full of forgiveness. She has even managed to pass on what she has learned to her mother and her siblings, and they have also each been given the gift of learning how forgiveness can change their lives. They have become a closer family and are working together to release the past.

Angela checks in with me every month or two to have a quick chakra scan. She likes to keep her chakras clean and balanced as part of her new holistic approach to living her life. When I see her, we discuss putting what she's learned about forgiveness into other aspects of her life with all the issues that come along as they do for all of us in our day-to-day lives. When we meet, we talk about the intense power her thoughts have and how she has the ability to keep herself well by consciously changing any negative thought patterns into positive ones. And of course, she continues to practice forgiveness each and every day.

"I believe that the very purpose of our life is to seek happiness. That is clear. Whether one believes in religion or not, whether one believes in this religion or that religion, we all are seeking something better in life. So, I think, the very motion of our life is towards happiness."
~ Dalai Lama

Chapter 3

Why I Believe What I Believe

I am the middle of three children. My brother is four years older than me, and my sister is two years younger. We grew up in a beautiful home with loving parents. We were given more than we needed materially, and we always knew we were loved, protected and safe. We had a comfortable life in a middle-class neighborhood where we attended good public schools.

I had a beautiful childhood full of all the childhood wonder that those who are blessed experience. I believed in Santa Claus, the Easter Bunny, the Tooth Fairy and even little green Leprechauns for a while! I remember that exciting feeling of butterflies in my stomach while waiting to put on my Halloween costume and go out trick-or-treating in my neighborhood, rushing through dinner thinking eating quickly would make the time go faster.

My mom's favorite holiday was Christmas. Each year the day after Thanksgiving she would begin to transform our home into a magical wonderland that continued for weeks. On Christmas morning, my little sister and I would wake up very early and first attempt to pry our older brother out of bed. Whether or not that was a success, (usually not) we would run into my parents' room to tell them what they already clearly knew; it was Christmas morning! My parents seemed to enjoy watching us open our many gifts as much as we enjoyed receiving them. Every gift had been picked out with much thought and care.

My mom would drag my dad to the mall night after night before Christmas shopping for the perfect gifts for each of us. Magical doesn't even adequately express how that time each year felt to me. These are precious memories given to me by my parents that are more significant and longer lasting than any present under the tree.

February would then come along. I loved making my Valentine's Day box out of glitter, tissue paper, and cut-out construction paper hearts. I remember every year my dad helping me create this little faux mailbox. I would proudly take my shiny, glittery shoebox to school where on the 14th all the children would exchange Valentines by putting envelopes with cards in the decorated boxes we had each so carefully created.

When summer came around each year, my mom and dad took us on wonderful vacations that were usually two weeks long. We visited all the attractions that Florida has to offer including the sandy beaches and of course Disney World. We vacationed in Virginia, the shores of New Jersey, Maryland, North and South Carolina and many other destinations. We would have great experiences and create lifelong memories wherever we went. We would get to swim in the ocean and play around in the pool at a lovely hotel that was sure to be right on the beach or boardwalk.

Even with all of those beautiful childhood experiences my very best memories came from a secret relationship I had with these beings I knew of as angels. Angels were always with me throughout my early years. They were part of my childhood; part of my life. The angels were my friends, playmates, protectors and my inspiration. They made me feel safe and comforted. Late at night when the house was quiet and long after my daddy had checked under the bed and in my closet for monsters multiple times I knew the angels were there taking care of me. I knew because I saw them, I sensed them, and I heard them. I could have conversations with the angels without saying a word out loud if. Instead, we would exchange thoughts. I was never afraid when they appeared. I knew they were magical, and I knew they were sent from Heaven.

The angels showed themselves to me as stunningly beautiful beings but also somewhat human looking. They were slightly iridescent with the most beautiful wings. Shades of light framed each of them with a faint but also distinct color. They radiated with the soothing essence of grace and peace. The angels sparkled and glowed with a brilliant light and energy.

I would often find secret hiding spots in my house to communicate with them in private. I didn't often have actual out-loud conversations with them. When we talked through thoughts, I'm sure it was noticeable to the people around me that something was going on. I was never good at showing a "poker face" and quite honestly I'm still not. When I was talking with the angels in thoughts, people were looking at me we wondering what was going on in that little head of mine because of my facial expressions. So I liked to hide. A favorite spot was my small walk-in closet. I had created quite a little retreat in that small space with pillows and blankets to lie with and books to read. I would sit in there for hours at a time with the light on and the door closed. Mostly I just exchanged thoughts with the angels but often I would read one of my many children's books to them. They always sat with me and tenderly listened. Eventually someone would come looking for me to join the family at the dinner table, and I would leave my quiet sanctuary for a while.

I remember thinking my awareness that the angels were with me was special, but I never thought it was strange or unusual and certainly never scary. I was very aware that everyone couldn't see and hear what I did, but never for a moment was I concerned about that. I knew I was safe; I knew I was loved, and I knew the angels were pure good. Even at a very young age I recognized what I was experiencing was miraculous.

Somewhere around ten years old I stopped being able to visually see angels in a physical form. I don't know why. Maybe I was too busy being a ten-year-old to realize what a gift it was to have this ability to see these messengers from God and I began to ignore their visits. Or maybe I became jaded as children do as they grow up and stopped believing what I was seeing. I'm not sure what happened because I don't remember the specific moment or day. But even after I couldn't physically see them anymore, the communication always continued. I still knew they were there. I felt them, and I continued to hear each thought they sent me. I still received their messages and their guidance when I asked for help. I was never without their protection. And often if it was dark and I asked for them, I could see sparkling lights when they came near. I sometimes still see their lights to this day.

But there was more than even the relationship with the angels in my world. I knew things that most people didn't know. Beautiful things! I knew there was a place where people went when their physical bodies died. I knew there were people that had passed before them waiting there to be reunited with them. I knew how this place looked. I knew we could change our appearance when we were there and change our environment with just a thought or wish. I knew there was a Creator who was called God that had arranged all of this. I didn't think of God as a person but more as everything good in the world all put together as one incredible force of loving, powerful energy. Some might think this was all just the active imagination of a child, but I always knew it was very real, and all of these beliefs continued long after my childhood ended. I never made a connection strangely enough between the angels and church or even religion.

Another memory I have is of being a small child of maybe six or seven sitting on my maternal grandmother's lap in a big rocking chair as she read to me from the Bible. She would tell me stories about God and Jesus and explain that I needed to be a good girl, say my prayers every night before bed, go to church and to Sunday School and obey the Ten Commandments. If I didn't do all of these things, I was told I could be cast into a horrible place called "Hell" where God might send me to be punished. My grandmother's description of Hell was not a place I ever wanted to see! I know now as an adult my grandmother wasn't trying to scare me by telling me this. She had been raised with this belief system and was attempting to protect me using what she had been taught. But even at this very young age, I stubbornly told my grandmother (who would quickly call my grandfather into the room for back-up) that I didn't believe God would do something mean like send someone to a horrible place like Hell just for making a mistake. That idea just didn't resonate well with me as a six-year-old. Of course questioning my grandparents' interpretation of the Bible was certainly not something that they appreciated or understood so I quickly learned to keep my opinions to myself. And when it comes to subjects of God, spirituality, religion or politics, I still hold to that same philosophy I also grew up with a peculiar, strong desire to be close to people who weren't feeling well, who were sick, or sad. I had a need to just touch them by rubbing their back or arm or holding their hand. This was another odd part of my early years. I had no idea why I needed to do this. Most people were keeping far away from someone that was ill in case they were contagious. But I just wanted to be near them. If I ever thought about it at all which I don't think I often did, I assumed I just felt sorry for them or was worried and wanted to offer comfort. Not coincidentally I'm sure until I was 14 years old my dream was to be a doctor; a pediatrician to be precise. I excitedly explained to my parents my plan to have an office that was built to look like a gingerbread house. I would ramble on telling them that I would be giving my little patients stuffed animals instead of stickers and lollipops. In retrospect, that seems to be the first noticeable sign that I wanted to be a healer.

I spent the first 13 years of my life living in Ohio. That was during the late 60's and through the 70's. We lived in a suburb of Youngstown. My dad was a successful salesman for a well-known cash register company and moved up the ladder fast to management. Eventually with one of the promotions he received came a transfer. So we packed our things and moved to a suburb of Philadelphia, Pennsylvania in 1979.

As most people do, I grew up, went to school, got a job, got married, had children and got divorced. (Okay, maybe *most* of us don't get divorced.) It was right around then I started realizing that I wasn't as "normal" as I was trying to be or maybe was pretending to be. I started looking back at my life with a microscope. I don't think it was any one event that caused me to start looking at my earlier life. It was more than likely a combination of events. My divorce, being a single mom of two small children, starting over and turning 30 all contributed. It was during this time I began analyzing my life. Why had everyone always come to me with their problems and sad stories? Throughout my life friends would say, "Lisa will know what to do.", "Lisa will make me feel better.", or "Lisa will know how to fix this." Now looking back on my life from the perspective of a thirty-something-year-old, I realized I always DID know what to do, how to make someone feel better or how to fix the problem. I just knew! At the same time, I also recognized that it wasn't just with my friends and family that I could sense the right and wrong moves but also with my own life. I thought about all the bad decisions I had made as a teenager and young adult, and I realized I had had a nagging gut feeling I was making a mistake before I made the actual mistake at the time. Unfortunately, as I explained earlier, it was a feeling I had ignored in many cases but still it had been there, and it had been intense.

So now I was faced with these questions: Why had I had this rare relationship with angels? Why had I known as a six-year-old child and probably even earlier that God and Jesus weren't the vengeful beings I should fear like my grandparents had told me? Why could I see in my mind an afterlife I thought of as "Heaven" as clearly as I could picture the furniture inside my bedroom? Why was it that when someone was sick I wanted to be close to them, to touch them and to feel that my touch was in some way helping? Why had I been desperately trying to rush through my life so I could get back to where I thought I belonged and where I longed to be? A place that I had regular dreams about that felt like real "home" to me?

I finally found many of my answers after doing months and months of deep soul searching, and then digging in and doing some research on my family history. I learned that I did indeed have some "gifts". I learned that my "just knowing" was one of those gifts, and it even had a name; a psychic ability known as claircognizance. I also discovered that I was a natural healer. And I wasn't a fluke! Other family members had gifts too. I was told about my great-great-grandmother (on my father's side) who was a very powerful psychic with many gifts including the ability to move objects with her mind that is called Telekinesis or Psychokinesis. The granddaughter of this astonishing woman was my grandmother who as I mentioned in the Preface just this year passed away at 100 years old. I'm incredibly grateful to my grandmother for having journaled for me all of her childhood memories so that I will always have her words verbatim explaining the many talents her grandmother possessed. The deeper I researched, the more I learned that there are other members of the family who have special gifts too.

It was at this point my life began an incredible transformation. After being divorced for several years, I met and married my husband, Scott. With that marriage, I became not only the mother of a caring and loving son and a witty, wonderful daughter from my first marriage but now I was a stepmother to another beautiful daughter. With the loving support of my family, I was able to begin a new chapter in my life concentrating on my true calling that involved using my God-given gifts whole heart, soul, focus and time into my family and my studies in Metaphysical Science and learn who I really was as a soul. I had finally found true happiness and inner peace. I am one of those very blessed individuals who now know my life's real purpose. I'm doing what I'm supposed to be doing. I now know I am here on this planet right now at this particular time to help others through guiding and healing. I am honored to have been chosen for the job!

So why do I believe what I believe? *I just believe.*

"We must be willing to let go of the life we have planned,
so as to have the life that is waiting for us."
~ Joseph Campbell

Chapter 4

What Is a Lightworker and Are You One?

Lightworker is a term that has been around for about 40 years. I define a lightworker as a person who is trying to transform human consciousness. These individuals have "awoken" or are in the process of awakening spiritually and are now connecting to their inner knowledge or higher self. And while lightworkers are developing and growing within, they are helping to influence others so they too can begin their awakening process. Lightworkers simply vibrate at a higher frequency and are much of the time, unknowingly affecting the people with whom they are in contact. A lightworker's vibration is very high and radiates with positive, bright, pure energy.

Lightworkers who are walking among us presently chose to incarnate now in this role when so many people on the planet are in need of guidance and leadership. When these souls were just that, souls on the spiritual plane before they were born into the human body they now inhabit, they made a decision to become a leader, teacher and/or a healer during this intense time of transformation. They have skillfully and masterfully trained for what is to come for them as human lightworkers. The lightworkers we are meeting now whether we seek them out for guidance or meet during our daily lives are souls that have been through suffering and trauma. Sometimes in a past life, sometimes in this life even both. Their suffering prepared their souls for the awakening they have experienced already or are now in the process of experiencing. In some cases during this lifetime but several years ago, they may have felt very disconnected physically, emotionally and spiritually and are just now finding a way to honor their true life purpose. Many are healers, gifted psychics, teachers, coaches, artists, writers and creative, sensitive individuals in other jobs that have been given an opportunity to initiate change within their lives and the lives of others.

There is no Earthly training to become a lightworker. If you are a lightworker, the training has already taken place before you were born. You just may not yet know it. If you feel you may be a lightworker and want to know more, you can learn more about them and what they do for the world and then begin to work on your inner gifts and abilities. As your soul becomes aware of who you are beyond all the Earthly "stuff", your awakening process can begin. This awakening will affect your life and the lives of the people around you. Most importantly you can start to listen to your higher self, that inner voice, your intuition that leads you to take the right path each and every time you listen.

Could you be a lightworker? Let me describe some of the characteristics of lightworkers that may resonate with you and help you to determine if you are in fact in the midst of a spiritual awakening or have already experienced one.

Lightworkers usually have spiritual, physical and emotional symptoms before and during their awakening. It is true that someone can have a much harder time dealing with the physical symptoms rather than the spiritual symptoms and conversely. No two lightworkers have the same experiences so you cannot expect to check symptoms off in a box like you might for a medical diagnosis to ascertain whether this is or is not what you are experiencing.

Lightworkers experience many spiritual symptoms. They might find they are very intuitive and highly sensitive. Many may feel they are empathic and able to pick up on the emotions of others effortlessly. Many feel out of place in this life or experience a feeling similar to being homesick. They often just don't feel at "home" here on this planet. Some will feel the need to do something more with their lives than what they are doing currently. I hear this often from my clients. They are not satisfied that they are making a big enough difference in the world with the work they do now and they want that to change. They may be looking for an entirely new career.

Other signs are very physical. For example changing sleep patterns, restlessness and sleepiness during the day. You may feel tingling or itching on you scalp (crown chakra) or energy surges in this area. Many people also experience this same sensitivity in their hands and up and down their spine. Changes in body weight can be another indicator. This can be a gain or loss that you do not feel you have initiated. There are many other physical symptoms like blurry vision, seeing shimmering objects, noticing colors around people, pets, plants or trees. You may physically see more intense colors everywhere; the sky may look bluer and the grass greener. Even your hearing could be affected and become a bit more sensitive. You may hear a high-pitched tone in one or both ears and so on. If you have any of these symptoms the first thing you should do is rule out any real medical condition with your doctor.

Some signs are emotional – such as crying for reasons you don't understand. A sudden onset of anger or sadness is a common side effect. Vivid dreams that are incredibly realistic or even sometimes paralyzing may also be experienced. Seeing repeating number sequences like 1111, 111, 222, 333, etc. is a very prevalent sign that you are receiving messages from angels. Another common occurrence is to have an issue from the past suddenly come up that causes you to be forced to deal with something you had buried deep within yourself.

There are hundreds of examples, but these can be researched on the internet or in books that focus on spiritual awakenings or lightworker symptoms. The most important thing to know is that lightworkers are here to help. You can trust them to know the correct path when it comes to spiritual issues, metaphysical subjects, psychic phenomenon and other aspects of life.

If you are a lightworker or suspect that you might be, understand that you are blessed. You've been given an incredible gift. You have been chosen as a soul who is spiritually advanced enough and strong enough to handle your awakening and the responsibility that comes with it. If you still require direction or assistance you can find a more experienced lightworker to help you with your symptoms and guide you. These more experienced lightworkers can usually be found teaching classes, writing articles and books and offering guidance, and healing in spiritual centers and practices around the world. Each of us has our individual purpose for being here. Lightworkers are meant to assist others in their spiritual advancement on a soul level. We are here to help in the awakening of others. We are waiting to help you so please reach out and take that first step to start developing yourself as a spiritual being.

"The secret of health for both mind and body is not to mourn for the past, worry about the future, or anticipate troubles, but to live in the present moment wisely and earnestly". ~Siddhartha

Chapter 5

What the Heck Is A Chakra?

The word chakra comes from the Sanskrit word meaning "wheel" but it is more accurately translated as "spinning wheel". The word chakra is pronounced "chuhk-*ruh*". Although chakra is a commonly used word for me, I can't help but laugh whenever I use it without even thinking about it and get a confused look on the face of the person with whom I'm speaking. Sometimes they choose to ignore me pretending they know what the word means or more often they ask me "what heck is a chakra?" (usually, pronouncing it wrong). I often forget that many people in the world have never heard this word. But I'm always happy to explain what the chakra system is to anyone who wants to know more.

At the central core of our body spin seven main wheel-like energy centers called chakras running along the spine. Chakras are energy vortexes that have the ability to receive, assimilate and transmit energy. There are seven major chakras connected to and part of the physical body. All of the seven main chakras are located on the torso and head. Each chakra transmits and receives life-force energy also called "chi" or "prana."

Over time with our daily life experiences, chakras tend to become clogged and muddied. When we are in a state of ill health, the chakras may become distorted, out of alignment or even stagnant. When this happens, life force energy cannot flow freely, and the physical body may suffer. Stress, inability to express emotions, overly emotional expression, disconnection from our higher power, over connection to religious beliefs, unhealthy diet, lack of exercise, exposure to toxicity and so much more can cause the chakra system to close down.

Every chakra corresponds to different organs, emotions and functions in the body. If you are feeling "off", imbalanced, sick, tired or just not at optimum health, your chakras need to be realigned and balanced. I believe chakra cleansings are one of the most important things I do for a client. Aligning and cleaning a person's chakras is so important it is often the first thing I do after an initial conversation during a session. I use Reiki healing, color therapy, aromatherapy, crystal therapy and meditation or a combination of several of these techniques if necessary for the cleansing.

Because the seven chakras are in a column from the base of the spine to the top of the head, they relate to one another. One chakra becoming unbalanced can affect the chakras adjacent to it as well. The energy transmission begins with the root chakra that is located at the base of your spine and flows upwards to the crown chakra that is at the very top of your head. If one of the chakras is muddied, the energy going to the next chakra will not flow correctly. Let's imagine your root chakra is muddied or clogged completely. The energy going to the six chakras above the root will not be the pure, healthy energy it should be. Root chakra problems are prevalent in many of my clients. Many times this is what brings them to me. They are not feeling well and are having no real luck with medical doctors diagnosing what is wrong.

Chakras get unbalanced by our life experiences. All our positive and negative experiences affect our chakras. Negative experiences can manifest themselves physically as health problems and disease. Because the chakras affect not only our physical well-being but also our emotional and spiritual well-being, the mind, body and spirit can be affected by dis-functioning chakras. So the holistic mind, body and spirit approach to healing is the perfect way to correct the issue.

The chakras are each a different color and spin at a different speed. The lower chakras spin slower than, the higher chakras. All of our chakras spin in a clockwise direction lying in a horizontal position. Each chakra also has a different area of your life to which it corresponds. For example, the lower chakras are attached to the material world while the higher chakras are attached to the spiritual world. Physical associations are also made. For example, the root chakra is associated with the kidneys, bladder, reproductive organs, vertebral column, hips, and legs while the crown chakra is related to the brain and its functions.

Ideally your chakras are each approximately the same size and clean, not muddied or clogged. Chakra clearing allows the balancing of all of your chakras so that they are all perfect in size, bright in color and spinning at the appropriate speed. There are many ways in which we can balance our chakras. Chakra therapy is enormously important to keep your energy flowing without restrictions throughout your body and subsequently keep you at optimum physical, emotional and spiritual health.

Below I have listed information on each of the seven major chakras including their color, position and function. This will give you an idea of what each chakras role is within the human body. At the end of this chapter, you will find a color diagram that will help you discern the different energy centers.

Base (Root) Chakra)

Meaning: I am

Color: Red

Position: base of the spine

Main Functions: survival, security, primal energy, will to live, connection to Earth, reflexes, shelter, endurance, confidence, basic trust, persistence, good judgment

Physical Dysfunctions: lower back pain, sciatica, varicose veins, depression, immune-related disorders, osteoporosis, problems with legs and feet, blood pressure, bowel disease, constipation, diarrhea, blood diseases, anemia

Mental and Emotional Issues: survival, cynicism, self- esteem, social order, security, family, depression, addictions, uncertainty, confidence, inability to handle stress, existential fears, trust issues, phobias

Related Organs/Body Parts: spinal column, kidneys, bladder, hips, legs, and feet

Sacral Chakra

Meaning: I feel

Color: Orange

Position: midway between the naval and base of the spine

Main Functions: relationships, sexuality, intimacy, sensuality, joy of life, creativity, confidence, enthusiasm

Physical Dysfunctions: low back pain, sciatica, fertility problems, hip pain kidney disease, menstrual problems, pelvic pain, libido, urinary problems, bladder problems, prostate and testicular disorders

Mental and Emotional Issues: blame, guilt, jealousy, inability to enjoy life, sex, power, control, lack of motivation, creativity, morality, sex addiction, risk of addiction, impulsiveness, sexual disinterest, severe mood swings

Related Organs/Body Parts: uterus, large bowel, prostate, ovaries, testes

Solar Plexus Chakra

Meaning: I do

Color: Yellow

Position: directly behind the navel

Main Functions: desire, vitality, inner strength, self-control, energy, sensitivity, compassion, sleep, confidence, intuitiveness

Physical Dysfunctions: stomach ulcers, intestinal tumors, diabetes, indigestion, anorexia or bulimia, hepatitis, cirrhosis, arthritis, jaundice, overweight, stomach disease, liver, spleen and gall bladder, heartburn, overall bad health

Mental and Emotional Issues: self-esteem, fear of rejection, apathy, oversensitivity to criticism, self-image fears, indecisiveness, self-awareness, ambition, emotional coldness, obsession for power, recklessness, tantrums

Related Organs/Body Parts: liver, spleen, stomach and small intestines, abdomen, gallbladder, middle spine, kidney, adrenals, overall health, eating disorders, sleep disorders

Heart Chakra

Meaning: I love

Color: Green

Position: center of the chest

Main Functions: release emotionally suppressed trauma, soul, and heart consciousness, expressing love, compassion, empathy, tolerance, deep understanding

Physical Dysfunctions: heart conditions, asthma, lung & breast cancers, pneumonia, upper back and shoulder problems, skin diseases, frequent colds, allergies, low or high blood pressure, coronary heart disease, high cholesterol levels, breathing problems

Mental and Emotional Issues: love, compassion, hope, confidence, inspiration, despair, hate, fear, jealousy, anger, generosity, bitterness, loneliness, relationship issues, coldness

Related Organs/Body Parts: heart, circulatory system, blood, lungs, diaphragm, thymus, breasts, esophagus, arms and hands

Throat Chakra

Meaning: I speak

Color: Blue

Position: throat

Main Functions: ability to verbalize, communication, speaking your truth, creativity, good voice, sense of humor

Physical Dysfunctions: sore throat, mouth ulcers, TMJ, swollen glands, hoarseness, neck and shoulder problems, thyroid dysfunctions, voice problems, laryngitis, tooth problems

Mental and Emotional Issues: personal expression, creativity, criticism, faith, will, lack of authority, inhibition, nervousness, shyness, language disorders like stuttering, etc.

Related Organs/Body Parts: throat, thyroid, mouth, teeth, esophagus

Third Eye (Brow) Chakra

Meaning: I see

Color: Indigo

Position: between the eyes

Main Functions: intuition, balanced state of mind, divine perfection, clairvoyance, memory, extrasensory perceptions, fantasizing, self-insight, mental clarity, imagination, insight to higher realities, concentration

Physical Dysfunctions: brain tumors, strokes, blindness and other eye problems, deafness, brain disease, migraines, schizophrenia, headaches, sinus infections, neurological issues, ear problems, seizures, learning disabilities, spinal dysfunctions, panic, depression

Mental and Emotional Issues: fear of truth, discipline, judgment, evaluation, emotional intelligence, concept of reality, confusion, concentration problems, restless mind, superstition, hallucinations

Related Organs/Body Parts: eyes, ears, sinuses, brain, neurological system, pituitary, and pineal glands

Crown Chakra

Meaning: I understand

Color: Violet

Position: top of the head

Main Functions: personal identification with infinite, oneness with God, inner peace, wisdom, divine guidance, spiritual understanding, self-expression

Physical Dysfunctions: diseases of the muscular or skeletal systems, skin issues, exhaustion, sensitivity to light, sound or environment, nervous disorders, Multiple Sclerosis, cancer, sleep disorders

Mental and Emotional Issues: discovery of the divine, lack of purpose, trust, selflessness, ability to see the bigger picture, devotion, inspiration, values, ethics, fixation on material world, lack of feelings, mental exhaustion, emptiness

Related Organs/Body Parts: top center head

As you can see, our chakras control everything in our bodies physically, emotionally and spiritually. Living our day-to-day lives takes its toll on us, and we need to think about the damage that is then done to us physically. Keeping your chakras balanced will help you live your life to your greatest potential and ensure that you stay healthy physically, emotionally and spiritually.

Most people can't perceive these seven energy centers with their physical eye. I have been given the ability to intuitively see the chakras and how those chakras interact to create the aura. Your aura can now be photographed with the use of Kirlian photography. I perform scans on my clients and am then able to clear and balance their chakras using my healing abilities and Reiki. If I had a Kirlian camera system, I could photograph a client before a chakra healing and then after to see the change in their aura.

I've witnessed this before, and the change is significant.

You can keep your chakras balanced on your own too. There are many fantastic meditations and visualization exercises that you can do specifically for chakra clearing and balancing. You don't need a special ability or gift to keep your energy centers working properly. Knowledge and practice will help a great deal when it comes to first becoming and then staying healthy.

The Chakra System

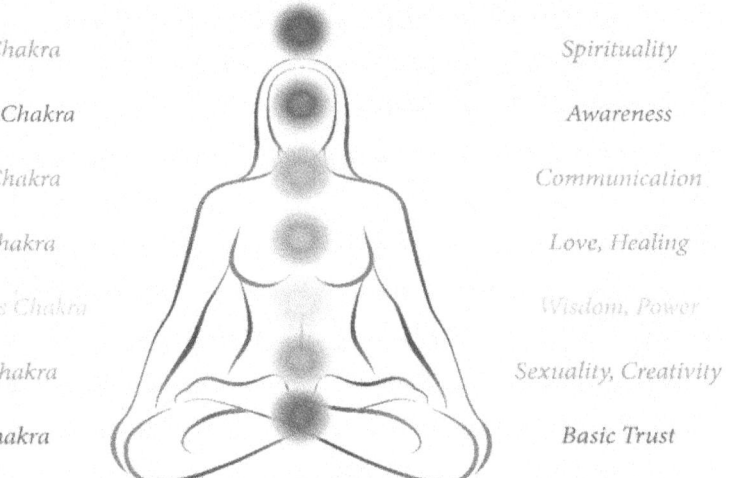

Crown Chakra — Spirituality
Third Eye Chakra — Awareness
Throat Chakra — Communication
Heart Chakra — Love, Healing
Solar Plexus Chakra — Wisdom, Power
Sacral Chakra — Sexuality, Creativity
Root Chakra — Basic Trust

"Never waste your time trying to explain who you are to people who are committed to misunderstanding you."
~ Dream Hampton

Chapter 6

Living as an Empath

If there's a psychic gift in existence that people would return if they could, it would be empathic ability. An empath is a person who is very tuned into the emotions of others. It is a psychic ability and from what I've been noticing the last ten or so years, not an uncommon one. Many of the clients I work with come to me with symptoms, traits and characteristics of someone with an empathic gift.

An empath can sense the emotions of others. They can feel anger, frustration, pain or any emotion in a stranger, friend or loved one when they are near them. When it's someone that they love, they may be able to pick up on the emotions or state of mind of that person no matter how far away they are geographically. Those with empathic abilities often have a very difficult time functioning especially in crowds. Many are prone to anxiety attacks, depression, and other emotional disorders.

I have had empathic abilities since the earliest I can remember. I was an extremely sensitive child unable to handle anyone being upset with me or fighting around me. My parents told me when I was older that when I was young and needed to be disciplined, they had to take me outside because I would always throw up. Luckily I was a pretty well-behaved child, or our neighbors would have thought my parents were pretty awful! Dealing with the intense emotions that come with grade school and beyond was very difficult. When my parents would take our family to crowded amusements parks, I often felt that I was outside of my body watching myself moving through the hordes of people. As recently as a couple of years ago I went to a local horse show and found myself sitting on a bench with my head down on my knees calming myself from an oncoming anxiety attack. I can tell you first hand this gift can be incredibly debilitating.

My empathic abilities have increased over the years and thankfully I have learned to cope by protecting myself with divine light and for the most part avoiding crowded places. I don't go near the mall at Christmastime. I avoid hospitals as much as possible. I don't go to amusement parks, local fairs or concerts with just a few exceptions anymore. With these crowds of people comes their emotions, and those can quickly become overwhelming. Even when the emotions are positive, in large groups, it's still very overpowering. Because people throughout my life began to notice this issue with me, I started to explain it away as my being claustrophobic that is a fear of small, confining places. Claustrophobia is a term most people understand and can relate with, so they don't ask questions.

In situations when I'm caught off guard by an intense wave of emotion because of a situation I'm in, I can become very quiet and come across as if something is suddenly drastically wrong. I know I am at my absolute limit when I get that same feeling I did as a child at an amusement park and feel my consciousness leave my body. At that point, I know I absolutely must remove myself from whatever circumstance I am in immediately.

The most important thing an empath can do is to avoid situations they know will prompt anxiety or stress because of the powerful emotions surrounding them. They should also always remember to protect themselves with light when they must be in a trigger situation. If they can't avoid it or have trouble someplace they didn't expect to have an issue, they can do what I call "throwing" protective light around them. This means to visualize a dome of light coming down from above and sealing in their energy and then protecting them from other energies reaching them.

Many years ago, I asked the angels to put a permanent light around me that will protect me from the emotions of others in addition to illnesses from clients when I'm doing counseling and healing work. However when I'm going out into the public, I ask for another layer of light to protect me as well. I personally choose different colors of light for different situations. For example, my permanent protective light is white.

If I'm going out and will be around a group of people, I will add an additional layer of gold light. If I'm feeling especially vulnerable for whatever reason, I then ask for a layer of violet light to surround me as well. To me, it's as common as putting my makeup on when going out.

You can do this too. Ask God, the Universe or the angels to surround you with light and then visualize it happening. I picture it coming from Spirit (God) into my crown chakra and surrounding my body. It's an amazing way of protecting yourself from negative energy and avoiding all the emotions that are not your own. You cannot live a very satisfying life in isolation. If you discover you are an empath, you should find a way to shield and protect yourself.

That brings me to the next part of this chapter. Could you be an empath? I know of many different "symptoms" that can help you answer that question. I have listed some of those below. However please remember this is a small list. There are many other symptoms. You don't have to have all of them to be an empath. You may be empathic and only have a few of these symptoms or traits.

- Empaths may block emotions to the point of seeming cold or unfeeling. This is the exact opposite of what you would expect and the opposite of what they are truly feeling.
- They may not like being touched by anyone even the people they love.
- Many are loners or avoid crowds in favor of smaller groups.
- Most empaths can sense how a person feels about them the second that they meet. If an empath can sense someone does not care for them, they will avoid that person at all cost.
- Many times empaths do not take care of themselves because they are so intensely concerned with the needs of others. The needs of other will always come before their own. It is not unusual for an empath to easily get colds, flus, and other illnesses.
- Empaths absolutely do not like situations that are intense. They will avoid arguments or circumstances where people are unhappy.

- Empaths do not like chaos and many times are bothered by too much noise. They are easily overstimulated with too much happening at the same time around them.

- Empaths can often pick up on the leftover energy from an argument or fight that has occurred before they even entered the situation. For example, if they are going to dinner at a friend's house, and that friend has a fight with their spouse earlier in the day, they can often still sense the tension even hours later upon entering the home.

- Many try to avoid watching or reading the news. They don't like to see others in pain or experiencing emotional trauma.

- They have a very hard time comprehending cruelty. They just don't understand or relate with why people are intentionally cruel to each other, animals or nature.

- Many empaths work as volunteers in their community.

- Empaths are known to be great listeners.

- They may tend to seem very moody.

- Empaths love deeply and often quickly. This can sometimes scare others away because of the intensity of their feelings and the quick onset as well as it setting the stage for their own heartbreak.

- Empaths are often creative people who enjoy things like music, cooking, art and writing.

- Empaths will find that people are attracted to them. Individuals naturally feel comfortable around them. Strangers may be very relaxed and at ease telling them their life story. People love to talk to an empath about their problems.

- Many empaths can sense the actual health of others including the existence of disease.

Although what I listed above are some common characteristics of empaths, many people don't know they have this gift until they are diagnosed with anxiety, depression, as bi-polar or with another mental illness. Many sense that the diagnosis is not right and begin to do some research. Although medication that may be prescribed can, in fact, relieve some of the symptoms, empathic ability is not an illness or disease that can be cured. Empaths can suffer long and hard because they do not understand what is going on within them or know that there is a way to protect them from the overwhelming emotions they live with that are not their own. Others don't accept a mental illness diagnosis given by a medical doctor or psychiatrist and go untreated living in isolation for long periods of time and sometimes throughout their entire life. If they do know what is going on, they can usually adjust their lives to make things easier for them to get through the issues they experience day-to-day.

Not only can an empath pick up on the energy and sensitivity of the living, but they are very likely to be able to sense energy from spirits.

This leads them to discover that they may have other psychic gifts. Empathic ability may just be the start of what they are capable of sensing or seeing. Empaths are so intensely sensitive to energy they are sometimes used by police personnel to help locate missing people and solve other crimes. This is because they can sense the emotional energy left behind at the scene where an abduction or a violent act has occurred and then follow that trail of energy.

Empaths may suddenly get very upset for no apparent reason only to find out later that someone they care about has been through some traumatic experience at that exact same time. They simply over-feel. This is why it is considered not only a gift but often a burden. It means living life where you are forced to experience your own emotional pain and also the pain of others. Unfortunately, empaths are often misunderstood by society because society doesn't understand them. They can be dramatic, loyal and very moral. They may be healers, speakers, poets, writers and have other forms of creative gifts.

Overall those possessing empathic ability can live amazingly positive fulfilling lives with the knowledge of what they can do comfortably and what they are not. As many negatives as I've talked about in this chapter, there is an inherent amazingness in having the ability to know when others need comfort and understanding. Empaths make for incredible caregivers, teacher, doctors, nurses, counselors as well as the many other things mentioned earlier. With understanding, they can learn to use their gift for the benefit of themselves and others around them.

"Don't judge me. You can't handle half of what I've dealt with. There's a reason I do the things I do; there's a reason I am who I am". ~ Unknown

Chapter 7

Judgment Sucks!

"Do not judge her. You don't know what storms I've asked her to walk through." - God

Something tells me that my readers will already sense how I feel about judgment in general by only reading the title of this chapter; am I right? I have never been good at mincing words. I'm a straight shooter, tell-it-like-it-is kind of girl. And here comes the truth as I see it about judgment.

Judgmental people have always slightly affronted me. These "judgers" think they know what is best for you and everyone else. They make sure you know the way you are handling any problems or circumstances in your life is entirely wrong. And the best part is, you don't even have to ask for their opinion. In fact, once you've recognized a judger as a judger you probably avoid telling them most issues that come up in your life or evade the person altogether. Even the positive things happening around you that you feel good about; the things you have made commonsense decisions knowing full well the consequences. Well, these people will seek out and somehow find the negative in the nooks and crannies of your life. They force their opinions and beliefs on you without you ever asking for their advice. The unfortunate part is they can make you feel a decision you made, something you know intuitively is the right one for you is wrong. You can quickly start self-doubting.

> *"Judge not, and you will not be judged; condemn not, and you will not be condemned; forgive, and you will be forgiven." - Luke 6:37*

Because of my strong feelings on this subject I felt the need first to define what judgment is. I needed to make sure my resentment over this behavior was not in fact the very act I was condemning! (Feel free to reread that sentence, I had to.) So I came up with my definition. I define judgment as: "an expression of distaste of another's decision out of righteousness". So what does that definition mean? A judger is a person who expresses their disagreement with your choices out of a feeling of superiority or an "I know more than you" type of mentality.

What they are so obviously missing is this: we all make our decisions based on our past and our personal life experiences. It's true that most people faced with the same situation would make different choices. Those decisions would be made based on their individual past experiences. There is no real right or wrong answer to many of the moral questions and queries we experience in our lives, just opinions. We do our best with what we know on an individual level. This as I mentioned in earlier chapters and will say again later in this chapter, is the way my parents and grandparents taught me and my siblings based on their past experiences. And I have and will continue that tradition with my children as I am sure they someday will with their children. We all make small changes and adjustments constructed from lessons we learn from our parent's mistakes and of course based on the fact that "times have changed". Yet in the end much of the basic lessons, morals and values remain the same.

> *"Do not speak evil against one another brothers. The one who speaks against a brother or judges his brother speaks evil against the law and judges the law. But if you judge the law, you are not a doer of the law but a judge. There is only one lawgiver and judge, he who is able to save and to destroy. But who are you to judge your neighbor?" – James 4:11-12*

When I began my research for this chapter, my first instinct was to look up how the Bible interprets judgment. The Bible is not normally the first avenue I take when looking for reference material. I sometimes find it complicated and outdated. But in this case, I was drawn to its interpretation. I was amazed at how many times the act of judgment is mentioned. This is a particular subject of the Bible that resonated well with me. I liked many of the verses throughout regarding judgment. I felt that they were similar to my feelings on the subject.

My personal belief is that judgment is something that should be reserved for our final life review with our Higher Power and then only for the judging of ourselves and how well we completed our life's purpose. Did we do our best to bring as much love and understanding as possible into the lives we touched? Did our lives serve a purpose and bring honor to our souls and our Creator? Were we at least successful in not harming anyone else?

> *"So put away all malice and all deceit and hypocrisy and envy and all slander. Like newborn infants, long for the pure spiritual milk, that by it you may grow up into salvation— if indeed you have tasted that the Lord is good. As you come to him, a living stone rejected by men but in the sight of God chosen and precious."* – 1 Peter 2:1-4

My issues with judgment have been with me since as early as I can remember. And although I have been guilty of the actual act on occasion as are most of us, it has always been something for which I have an incredible distaste when I witness it. I've asked myself on many occasions how anyone could know how they would react to a situation or problem that is not part of their actual existence? And why would a person feel they can righteously judge another unless there was something inside of themselves that needed attention or healing? The act of judging seems to be an act of resentment towards others. Resentment comes from fear, not love. Love and fear are the fundamental emotions that all other emotions are built. Judgment must then be based on fear.

> *"There is only one lawgiver and judge, he who is able to save and to destroy. But who are you to judge your neighbor?"* – James 4:12

A judgmental person is someone who chooses to express an unsolicited opinion as if they know a better way or "the right" way versus your way. In actuality, they can have no idea what they would do in another's particular situation. They cannot have lived a parallel life and, therefore, had identical past experiences. No one can know the decision they would make in any area of someone else's life without the benefit of walking every minute of every day in that person's shoes for the entirety of their life.

All of our victories, successes, mistakes, trials and tribulations make up the people we are today. Each of us is who we are because we are not perfect. We are all flawed. And really if we were all perfect wouldn't this be a boring world in which to exist? Wouldn't we all be exactly alike? Would we even know what perfection was since it would be the only thing we knew? There would be no variances, no debates, maybe even very little conversation.

I think it can be fairly simple for us to look at another's life from a lofty perch and say what we would or would not do in a similar set of circumstances. I struggled with this personally because of the work I do. I had to ask myself if I am judging others by guiding my clients on a path based on my education, intuitive and healing gifts and what I sense will be the healthiest and happiest option for them. Is that judgment? During my workday, I spend most of the time examining someone's physical and emotional health and evaluating if the way a particular person is living is working for their overall highest good. I look at their lives asking the question how is each of my client's mind, body, and spirit reacting to the choices they are making? If they are happy, healthy and living life to their fullest potential, they are probably not in my office. However, most of us need help and guidance at certain times of our lives minimally from family and friends and many times from a professional practitioner.

I finally reached the conclusion that my clients come to me only after they have judged their own lives. This is one type of judgment that is acceptable and understandable in my opinion. Even then, however, it should only take place with self-love and self-respect. When my clients come to me and ask for help, there is no judgment on my part; only pure love, real compassion, and all the healing energy I have to give.

Let's talk about bullies. This is another type of judger that is out there that is very dangerous. Bullies like judgers are also forcing their unsolicited opinions on others. In this case, it's a little different. They don't just have a personal debate with you and tell you how you didn't do things right or how they would have done them differently. Bullies usually function in groups where they have camaraderie. Many times they operate using violence whether through physical or verbal harassing behavior. This is what sets them apart and makes them much more dangerous than an ordinary judger. Bullies have so much internal pain they only know how to deal with their difficulties by attempting to make others feel pain too. They enjoy bringing people down to the same vibrational level in which they are functioning. It's mean, cruel and lacks any good personal character. Bullies are not usually connected spiritually and care only for their own selfish wants and needs.

Bullies urgently need to begin to examine their necessity to make others feel worthless. Where does this need come? What does a person get from this behavior that assists in helping them feel better if only for a moment here and there? There is so much permanent damage that can be done to a person by the actions of a bully.

Bullying needs to stop. *It must end!* Much inner soul work needs to be done to assist with the growth that has to take place within these individuals. What has gone so terribly wrong in someone's life that they feel good when inflicting pain in any way, shape or form on someone else? Bullies need to stop seeking attention by placing themselves center stage where they are often cheered on by the masses. Instead, they need to focus on their personal issues from their past that have resulted in unresolved pain, anger and lack of forgiveness. It needs to happen immediately before they do any serious damage to another person. If you know a bully, do what you can to safely get yourself or your affected loved one away from the situation. Involve people in authoritative positions if necessary. If you are a bully, please get professional help to stop this conduct. As bullies progress and grow as souls throughout their lifetime, they will hopefully see their behavior as very wrong. But the pain they've caused others is not something that can be undone. I believe that bullies are unhappy internally and not at all at peace with themselves. They have more than likely experienced bullying by someone else or another type of physical or emotional abuse in their lives that have yet to be healed. So this is where the initial examination should begin.

Lastly, there is a more subtle everyday type of judgment that most of us engage in at least some of the time but don't usually think of as a judgmental act. Early in my teenage years I noticed an attempt by my parents to shelter me from certain people and situations I didn't understand why. I wasn't forced to let go of existing friendships, but I did notice that my mom especially seemed to prefer certain friends over others. So as I did with most of the things that puzzled me during my childhood and teenage years, I put on my detective hat, pulled out my magnifying glass and Calabash pipe and did some detecting. (Obviously this is metaphorically speaking or at least that's the story I'm sticking to!) It was then I started to notice this fact: what neighborhood my friends lived in, what their parents did for a living, what their religion was and what I considered other superficial things seemed to really matter to my parents. I didn't understand why those things should make a difference to them when they certainly didn't to me.

And then there were the boys. My parents were obviously very cautious about who I dated like most parents of teenage girls. When I was 16, I was permitted to "car date" meaning go on a date with a boy who drove. Luckily by then my mom had gotten over some of her concerns especially regarding religious background. . I was lucky enough not to be limited to only dating Methodists, which had been mandatory for my mom when she was a teenager. But she was still attempting to control my choices especially the social aspects of my life. I wasn't comfortable with it. I felt many of her assessments were based on judgmental motives.

So as a teenager often does, I rebelled! And wow did I rebel! I stopped dating the nice boys, and I started dating the "bad boys". The type of boy that keeps a dad awake at night loading his shotgun. Yep, that's the one! THAT boy! I spent about four years doing everything I could to piss my parents off and make them see I wasn't going to be judgmental because of what I was deeming as superficial. I was fighting back!

Well I fought back and ended up becoming more and more miserable as time went on. Eventually, I stopped dating bad boys and started realizing that maybe my parents weren't as horrible as I thought. Was it possible that I didn't know absolutely everything about absolutely everything? (If you're over, say 21, you can probably remember that shocking moment in your life when you realized your parents weren't complete idiots!)

As the universe has a tendency to do, it spun me around and threw me right on my butt. I ended up married to a cop. How did I meet this cop? Well, I had to call the police on the last "bad boy" I dated. Funny story (last two words written with tons of sarcasm). I had a brand spanking new car and had allowed this "devoted" boyfriend to borrow it. The next day I walked out my front door to go to work and my car was not in front of my house as he had promised. When I called him about this, he insisted it must have been stolen. The police later found it smashed to pieces in a parking lot in the next town over. Oh, and it gets better. Being the trusting, naïve soul I was at the time, I allowed him to borrow the rental car my insurance company had given me while my car was being repaired. And again, he didn't bring it back. Shocking I know! Yes, he had pretty much stolen two cars from me within about three days. (I told you they were REALLY bad boys.) So, my parents and I finally united and called the police. Enter my first husband. So, to wrap it all up, we were married for seven years and had two fantastic children before we divorced. A few years later, I met and married my husband Scott and found the person with which I could build the life I wanted. He comfortably fits in my world of not a total "good" boy, but not a frightening "bad" boy either. We base decisions we make for our family on our past experiences including our first marriages. In some situations, I may not have the experience and my husband could very well be more knowledgeable in a particular area and vice versa. It's a balance within the relationship and our blended family.

As the years went by, I finally came to the realization that my parents' attempt to shelter me was, of course, their way of trying to protect me from the negative things in life they didn't think I needed to experience (like two stolen cars in a same week!). I finally grasped that my mom and dad had lovingly dedicated their lives to trying to protect their children and went out of their way to keep us safe physically and emotionally. As it turns out, it's the same way I would go about protecting my children. I can relate with this now as a parent.

However, the fact that judgment bothered me so much as a teenager caused me to be overly cautious to not judge my children's friends. But even with all this history and high emotion on the subject, I fell right into the judgment trap, hook, line and sinker.

I learned as a parent you just can't help but have thoughts creep up once in a while that put you on guard when it concerns your children. I found myself judging using methods I could explain away as just more "convenient". I would be insistent, especially in cases of sleepovers, that some of my kids' friends sleep at our house instead of my kids sleeping at that friend's house. If the family didn't live in what I felt was a safe neighborhood or have a "stable" family, I didn't want my kids staying there overnight. I would just explain that it would be more convenient for me if the children slept at my house. Suddenly I realized that seemed very similar to what my parents had done – only I thought I was a little slicker and subtle about it. I was acting judgmental. It was in an attempt to protect my children but still it was judgment.

All judgment is wrong and sucks, but we all do it from time to time in some form or another. That doesn't make us bad people just unsurprisingly imperfect. As long as we notice when we are committing the act of judgment, and we try to correct it, we are doing just fine. Judgment only hurts the feelings of others and certainly isn't created from a love based emotion. It's a fear-based emotion that becomes a fear-based action. We have the ability to keep our opinions, so our judgment to ourselves.

Just because it comes into our head doesn't mean it has to come out of our mouth. Let's remember that important God-given filter we have that stops us from saying and doing everything that pops into our head. We simply need to be aware of the negative thought when we feel it roaring its ugly head. Stop, think and remember that every one of us has imperfections. We are each very different because of our backgrounds and familiarities. In most situations, we are each doing the best we can based on what we know, what we have experienced and who we are as a person. Of course, there are exceptions when we have little choice but to get involved to protect others. However, we can still do that without being in a judgmental state of mind.

We are each here in this time and place to learn soul lessons, whatever they may be. We all need to respect the differences in each and every soul we come across throughout our lives. One way to do that is by keeping our opinions to ourselves unless we are asked for help and then and then only to give our support from a place of love.

> *"Do not judge me until you know me, do not underestimate me until you have challenged me, and do not talk about me until you have talked to me." – Unknown*

I'll end this chapter with the following phrase I came across a while back:

"Before you speak ask yourself if what you are going to say is true, is kind, is necessary and is helpful. If the answer is no, maybe what you are about to say should be left unsaid." - Bernard Meltzer

"Anyone can hold a grudge, but it takes a person with character to forgive. When you forgive, you release yourself from a painful burden. Forgiveness doesn't mean what happened was okay, and it doesn't mean that person should still be welcome in your life. It just means you have made peace with the pain and are ready to let go."
- Unknown.

Chapter 8

Forgiveness

"Forgiveness is not something we do for other people. We do it for ourselves – to get well and move on." – Unknown

I began this book with a true story about a client who needed to forgive her deceased father in order to allow her mind, body and spirit to heal from years of pain. I chose that story out of the hundreds of other encounters I've had because the power of forgiveness cannot be over emphasized. Forgiveness is without a doubt a practice that can change and will change your life forever in amazing and very positive ways. Forgiveness will keep you healthy both physically and emotionally. It can be an incredible cure when you are in a state of illness or disease. It is a type of treatment that requires no doctor, no prescription, and no money. You can take a dose of it any time you are ready as often as you like.

Growing up I could hold a grudge like nobody's business. I initially trusted everyone I met (as the last chapter may have illustrated regarding my stolen car(s) story). It came naturally. I knew I was trustworthy, so I assumed that everyone was the same as me. Of course, I learned that there are people like me out there, but there are more who just aren't like me at all. Unfortunately, there are many not so good hearted or trustworthy and honest people in the world. And when someone hurt me? God help the poor soul who did anything to lose my trust. They were angrily cast out of my life forever! My mom often told me throughout my childhood and through my twenties that I needed to learn how to forgive. She said holding onto all that anger for so long, (almost my entire life at that point) wasn't helping anyone. I wasn't hurting the person with whom I was angry. I was only damaging myself with the anger I carried inside me. I didn't comprehend what she meant when she said that I needed to forgive. How do you forgive someone for hurting you or betraying you? Didn't that, in fact, mean that I would have to believe what they did to cause me pain was okay if I were to forgive them?

Then I read *You Can Heal Your Life*, by Louise Hay, and it changed everything. I highly recommend anyone reading my book right now purchase this book next. It was required reading for a course I was taking for my Bachelor's Degree in Metaphysical Science. When I began reading it, I had no idea how much more it would end up being to me than just another "textbook". It was this book that I can say honestly changed my life. I was fascinated by it from the very second I saw the cover. I had the "gift edition" that is beautiful! I loved the way it looked, the way it was designed, the beautifully colored pictures and most of all the incredible wisdom that was covering all the pages.

Very early in the book, Part One, Chapter One, I found the following sentences and they changed my attitude: "Forgiveness means giving up, letting go. It has nothing to do with condoning behavior. It's just letting the whole thing go. We do not have to know how to forgive. All we need to do is be willing to forgive. The universe will take care of the hows."

Wow! Knock me over with a feather! I probably read and reread those words a hundred times. How could a small paragraph in one of the hundreds of books I'd read so far in my lifetime have this kind of influence on me? This was the issue I had struggled with my entire life. The answer was right there on one page in this book! It was as simple as these three little words: "LET IT GO"! Eventually, I realized its effect on me was so intense because it was *exactly* what I needed to hear. I needed someone to confirm for me that it wasn't okay that people had hurt me, cheated on me, betrayed me, used me and lied to me. And it was clearly explained I certainly wasn't expected to give them open access to my life and allow them permission to hurt me again. But in fact, what I was doing by forgiving them was saying they weren't getting another second of my time or energy. I was forgiving them. I was letting the whole thing go.

This had a profound effect on my personal life. But it was more than just that. It made so much sense to me that it took over much of my life in so many ways and became the most common thing I still to this very day teach. Harboring anger towards situations or people causes illness. It just makes us sick. Living in a state of unforgiveness means we're holding onto anger and pain. We are in fact allowing the person who hurt us to dictate our health and well-being not only right now, but into our infinite future. And a shorter miserable future it may end up being.

Each of us as individuals has to decide how healthy and fulfilled we want our lives to be. To be happy and healthy, we have to take back control of our emotions. Even ones we experienced in our past and maybe never completely dealt with for a variety of reasons. Actually moving on from a situation that caused us great pain must start and end with forgiving. When we no longer have anger or resentment in our hearts and only pure love and acceptance resides in that space, we're finally fully living our lives. We are truly balanced in mind, body and spirit.

So is this an easy task? Is forgiving someone as simple as I just made it sound? In fact in some situations it can be and in others it is more difficult. First we have to be willing to release the anger we are holding on to. Sometimes that anger is so much a part of us that releasing it feels like we are giving up a piece of ourselves. If that is true, it's a piece of ourselves that is only causing us damage. It's like having a splinter in your finger that agitates you by causing you pain and then eventually becomes a horrible infection but you never bothering to take the time to remove it from just under your skin's surface. We begin to release anger by recognizing that all humans are imperfect and in some cases even weak. We start by looking in the mirror and forgiving ourselves for any pain that we may have caused others in our lifetime. And since none of us is perfect, at some point in our lives we have indeed hurt someone else even if entirely unintentionally. First forgive yourself. Sit with that for a while. Feel how forgiveness feels. Feel how the tension in your body dissipates and the hole in your soul begins to mend. Then one by one (I actually made a physical list of the people I needed to forgive) forgive those who have caused you pain, hardship or anger by looking in your heart. Recognize that no one on this Earthly plane is perfect including you.

With that said it's important to remember that when the wound is still very fresh it's okay to allow yourself to go through the process of feeling the pain and the anger. It's okay and even healthy to feel the hurt, disappointment, grief, anger and resentment that are likely to come up during the early hours, days or weeks of the event. Allow yourself to process the pain. Don't bury it or hide it away. Feel it and understand what you are feeling is entirely normal. It's okay to spend some time licking your wounds and recovering. But what you need to do eventually no matter what you experienced and as soon as you are ready, is to *let it go*. Release the anger and release the person that caused it. You are not required to have a relationship with this person or even ever talk to them again if you choose, but you do need to allow your heart to release them and your soul to forgive.

It's important to repeat that in order to forgive others, you must forgive yourself. We are all imperfect creatures. There may be small differences in how quickly we trust or how vulnerable we allow ourselves to be, but all in all we are equal in that we each have our individual imperfections. And even with those imperfections we each deserve love and forgiveness for ourselves and each other.

"Respect yourself enough to walk away from anything that no longer serves you, grows you, or makes you happy." - Unknown

Chapter 9

Energy Vampires

"Don't worry about what people say behind your back. They are the people who are finding faults in your life instead of fixing the faults in their own life." – Unknown

The Energy or sometimes called Psychic Vampire is someone who exists in almost all of our lives. Many of us have more than one of them around. Worse yet we may not even know they're there. These Energy Vamps continually make us feel physically and emotionally exhausted even with just the smallest interactions.

An Energy Vampire is typically defined as a person who feeds off the "life force" of other living creatures. Energy Vampires are spiritually and emotionally weak people who because they are unable to generate their own life force, instead have to feed off of others. As long as these people are feeding on the positive, happy people around them they will save themselves from the physical and emotional symptoms they naturally experience such as depression, headaches, dizziness, irritability and anxiety. Unfortunately, an Energy Vampire's victim will have all of those difficulties as a result of the attack plus the added feeling of being drained and exhausted.

Energy Vampires exist because they are blocked in their connection with the Universe. Because of this disconnect they are forced to find other ways to get their energy. They do this through the people around them that are firmly connected to the Universe. Negative people are often labeled as Energy Vampires. Like a vampire feeds off of an individual's blood to survive Energy Vampires feed on the energy of others.

If you have ever encountered one of these Energy Vampires, and most of us have, they most certainly left you feeling drained, tired and lethargic. This is the type of person that no matter what you say while engaging in a conversation or how intensely you try and change their pattern of pessimism, they will always find a way to make any and every situation negative. Anytime they have a problem in their lives, instead of dealing with it rationally and productively, they like to wallow in it. One reason for this is because they like playing the role of a victim. These individuals are completely fixated on drama, doom, and gloom.

Energy Vampires also like to bring others over to their way of thinking. Once again let's compare to a vampire like we read about in books and see in movies. Like those type of vampires, the energy vampire likes to convert people to their way of living because of their loneliness and need for companionship. Remember the old saying misery likes company? This is especially true for the Energy Vampire. They feel better physically when they are spreading their unhappiness to others. It gives them a sense of camaraderie.

So how do you know if these vampires are in your life? Your Energy Vampires are the people you dread being near. You may find yourself avoiding any and all situations where you might see or have to interact with them. If you are forced to be in their company, you prepare yourself emotionally and possibly even physically. These are the people in your life who when their name comes up on your phone's caller id, you either roll your eyes dreading the phone call, or you just send them to voicemail. You can't find the strength to talk to them without time to prepare yourself. You know that your interaction with this person will cause your positive energy to be sucked away. Then you're left feeling lousy, exhausted and out of sorts for the rest of the day.

Energy Vampires take your positive energy and use it for their survival. They lower your energy vibration, so you begin feeling what they feel all the time; ashamed, angry, sad, frustrated and a bunch of other negative physical and emotional feelings. But when you take the time to think about it, before you had contact with them you were feeling happy, having a great day, radiating positivity and overall feeling pretty darn good. Then the light bulb comes on. You realize an Energy Vampire has just attacked you!

So what can you do? First figure out who the vamps in your life are. You can do that by making a list of all the people in your life. Start with those you deal with on a daily basis, and then weekly and finally less often. Next to each name add a word for how you feel when you have any interaction with them. Do you feel happy and positive? Does the interaction cause no change in your mood? Or do they leave you drained and terrible? You might choose to use words like "positive", "neutral" and "drained" next to their names. Once you have completed your list, look it over. Notice all the names where you wrote "drained" or whatever word you chose. These are no doubt your Energy Vampires.

So now what? You know who is causing the problem but what do you do about it? Best case scenario is you have the ability to cut these individuals out of your life completely. Decide for yourself if your relationship with each of these people is essential. Is this person perhaps someone you don't have to deal with anymore? For instance is it an acquaintance or co-worker that you can find a way to avoid? If that's the case, completely disconnect yourself from this person. Avoid them. Problem solved!

But what if this person is someone you have little to no choice but to deal with regularly? Maybe it's your boss, and you don't want to leave your job or a family member that you love. One option you have is to cut back on the amount of time you spend with them. This is especially true with one-on-one contact that is the most draining. Although you may not be able to cut them completely out of your life, you can certainly choose to limit the time you spend with them. Remember, we ultimately have control over our lives and who we allow into it. One-on-one in person contact is the most draining with an Energy Vampire.

Prepare yourself. Know when you see him or her it will most likely be a negative experience. Although you should always hope for the very best case where the vamp has realized their negativity is damaging to themselves and the people around them, most likely they are a going to have something negative to say to you or about you.

It's what they always seem to do. Another way of defending yourself that works for me is making a joke about what they say. You don't have to do this out loud if you don't want to, but think it. This will help the negativity to bounce off of you. Keep strong, use humor and just don't let them get to you. Most people have a hard time being negative if they are laughing.

You can also protect yourself from these vampires by picturing white or gold light surrounding you before you see them. Keep that light around you anytime you are in a situation where you usually see your vampire. To create this light, just envision it surrounding you from your head to your feet. This Universal protection will then be there engulfing you entirely. If you feel inclined, you may also ask Archangel Michael to protect you throughout your day and keep the Energy Vampires away from your positive energy.

Another situation many people experience is the Energy Vampire from their past. This is someone you are probably no longer communicating with in the present however they have linked themselves to you through an etheric cord (I will discuss etheric cords in detail in Chapter 14). An etheric cord severing is usually required to deal with this vampire.

When you research Energy Vampires on the internet, you will find there are between three and seven types mentioned. Below are the types I have been able to identify and come across in our day-to-day-day lives.

Vampire 1: Always Negative

These are the doom and gloom people in your life. No matter what you say, these people will find a negative way to spin it. You can tell them the happiest news, "I just won a million dollars!", and they will say something that will absolutely bring you down like, "Wow, I wouldn't want to have to pay those taxes". They have a way of finding the negative in every situation they come across. They are never happy. And for the rest of us, being in their presence can make us feel depressed. They usually have a dark cloud hanging over them and generally suffer from depression.

Vampire 2: Drama Lovers

The more drama surrounding these vampires, the happier they are. If there's nothing exciting going on around them to get involved with and talk about, they'll make something up. They are always hungry for gossip. Don't think you're off limits either just because they gossip to you about others. If they're gossiping to you, they are definitely gossiping about you. They will do anything they can to make waves and cause trouble. They love being the center of attention and feeling they know something others don't know. But, they will always be willing to share those secrets with even just subtle persuasion. They usually appear to be looking for attention in any form they can get it. The bigger the audience the harder they will try to get attention by starting trouble.

Vampire 3: The Controller

This vampire has an opinion about absolutely everything. There is nothing they can't tell you how to do. They think they know what's best for you and everyone else in every situation. They are very rigid in their definition of right and wrong and speak out about it. They like to make sure everything is done their way and very seldom want other's input about anything going on around them. Why would they need or want your input? They already know everything.

Vampire 4: The Criticizer

These people are the judgers. They feel they can belittle you and by doing so bolster their own ego. They make you feel small, unimportant and worthless. They have nothing positive to say about anyone or anything. Many times these people don't think before they speak and are prone to easily hurt the feelings of people with whom they are in contact. Being around them might make you feel depressed or even angry. They will no doubt leave you feeling drained and very unsure of yourself.

Vampire 5: Poor, Pitiful Me

These vampires have the saddest most depressing stories to tell you. There is never a day that they can't find a hundred things wrong with their lives. Remember that lottery I talked about with Vampire 1? Even if They were the one to win that million dollars in the lottery I was talking about before, this vampire will still feel sorry for themselves because they would have to figure out where to put all the cash (and, of course, the tax issue!). They are depressed and entirely negative. When you encounter this vamp, you will more than likely feel sorry for them immediately; they certainly can tell you all their sad woes. After a short amount of time with them, however, you will notice you just feel depressed and drained.

Whether the vampire is in your life presently or still attacking from a distance, they do not have the right to be in control of your life. As energetic beings with free will, we each get to decide who we allow into our lives and how we allow them to affect us. We can cut their energy supply off, and they will be forced to find energy elsewhere. Better yet they may finally look inside themselves to find the answer to their neediness and unhappiness. What matters most is each one of us as a part of this beautiful Universe is permitted to live our lives in peace and choose who and when we give of our energy.

"Being happy doesn't mean that everything is perfect. It means that you've decided to look beyond the imperfections." - Unknown

Chapter 10

Happiness Is Simply A Choice

"Happiness is a journey, not a destination." – Ben Sweetland

I love this part! Imagine your life always being awesome. You're always positive, and you live life to the fullest each and every day. Imagine yourself as one of those people who always sees the upside in everything. The people who are always in high spirits, smiling and glowing with radiance. We are all so mesmerized by these people we can't help but wonder what their secret is. Do they have billions of dollars stashed away somewhere and just keep picturing stacks of cash to make them this happy? Are they taking a great happy pill and not sharing? Are they completely phony or fake?

How are they doing it? How can these people always seem so freaking happy?

What would you say if I told you these people didn't have billions of dollars stashed away, there was no happy pill and that they were genuinely happy – no phoniness involved? What if I told you they had as many problems as you do or maybe even more? What if I told you they were just like the rest of us, but they had just one little secret? And best of all they aren't trying to keep it secret; they are willing to share it *for free*! Do you think I'm crazy? (Well if you do get in line, but that's really not the point.)

Even though that may have just sounded a little bit like an

infomercial, there is no need to worry. There is no catch. No 14-day money back guarantee. No five easy payments of $19.99 (+ shipping and handling). It is really simple to be happy. We just don't recognize what that one little secret is that some others know all about. So I'm going to share this secret with you. Are you ready? The secret is: it's a CHOICE you make. That's it!

Every day when you get out of bed you make a choice. You can choose to wallow in your problems and be miserable knowing things in your life aren't perfect or just aren't the way you "pictured" they would be. You can stress out about the fact that there is a stack of bills you can't pay and a job you don't want to go to not to mention all kinds of drama surrounding you. Or you can choose to look at all the beauty around you and the many gifts in your life and focus on those. You can actually choose to be HAPPY! If you decide to take the happy route, the bills are still going to be there, the job is still going to be a pain, and you'll still find drama around you. Either way happy or miserable those things are there. So ask yourself, "Am I going to be miserable and focus on the bad or am I going to be happy, thank God for all the gifts in my life, recognize that there are so many people in the world who have much bigger problems than mine and just choose to be happy?"

We don't realize it, but it is a physical, emotional and mental decision we make each and every day. We could have a list of problems a mile long but when we get up every morning, we can still choose to be happy in spite of those problems. Worrying and being stressed out about all the things that are wrong in your life doesn't help to create a solution. It only adds to the problem. Like attracts like, right?

Did that sound too simple? Just choose to be happy. Well, you are probably thinking, "That sounds great Lisa but let's get real here, where do I even start with something like that"? How do you change a pattern you've been living with for however many years, focusing and worrying about the bad stuff, and now just magically stop worrying and start focusing on the good? Well, don't you worry (get it??) I'm going to help you with the answer.

The only reason we are not all completely happy each and every day is because we choose to not let go of the things that make us sad. Think about that. I know I keep repeating this, but I have to tell you again: happiness REALLY is a choice. We can stop being unhappy by letting go of what makes us that way. All we have to do is make a conscious decision to let go of the things that keep us from complete happiness.

We spend more time worrying about all the negative things that could or might happen in our lives instead of focusing on the beautiful things already taking place all around us. There are so many miracles we see every day that we don't acknowledge because we've surrounded ourselves in a thick muddy mess of doom and gloom. The only way to leave the unhappy place we are in is by deciding where we want to go from here and then going for it! As the saying goes, "Worrying doesn't take away today's troubles, it only takes away today's peace". We need to spend our energy being grateful for those things that are wonderful in our lives and not spend any of our energy on the things that have already happened that we can't control or change. So many people just miss the good stuff in their lives because all they can focus on are the things that are going wrong or the things they don't have. Those destructive things have taken over. I'm not in any way trying to downplay financial problems, health issues and serious situations that are going on all over the world. I'm merely saying worrying and not living our lives in a happy state is letting the problems win. The problems shouldn't get to win.

So as the storms come in and out of our lives, and you know they will, instead of holding on and struggling, worrying and trying to fight your way through, try just letting go. Know that God will work you through the struggles you are experiencing. But, also remember He can't help until you stop fighting Him for control. Relax and let go of the control. Believe that things will work out for the best and recognize looking back at your life so far, most things have done just that. Somehow they always worked out in the end. Have faith in God and His plan and most importantly, do the thing He put you on this Earth to do: Love with everything you have and be happy.

"Millions of spiritual creatures walk the Earth unseen, both when we wake and when we sleep." ~ John Milton

Chapter 11

Angels and Spirit Guides

I reserved Chapter 11 for the angels and spirit guides section since the number 11 is directly linked to the angelic realm and the messages they send us. There is a lot of information available on what are called "angel numbers." I had a session with the angels where I asked them what each of the commonly seen numbers (1111, 111, 222, 333, etc.) mean. When the session was over, I compared my information with what other psychics who have had similar communications with angels had been told, and the results were quite similar. You can find these articles and websites all over when you search the internet for angel numbers.

As you read earlier, I have been blessed with having experiences with angels my entire life. It has been such a miraculous gift. I feel honored to have had them and continue to have them touch my life. I am optimistic and believe I will continue to have experiences with angelic beings throughout the rest of this life and of course beyond. I can't imagine my life without the company of angels.

Here's a very recent story you'll enjoy. After writing the beginning of this chapter, I found a good stopping point and decided to turn in for the night and get ready for bed. I turned off the lights making my bedroom completely dark which always happens at night since there are no streetlights in my neighborhood. The room was pitch-black for a second or two until suddenly it was filled with sparkling lights jumping everywhere. Immediately I received a message. The angels reassured me they were there with me always and then lovingly gave me their approval for what I had written already and what they knew I would write in the in my book but they never expect or even desire anything in return for their many gifts to us. I thanked the angels for coming to me and sending me the message. The lights slowly started to fade away as each angel began to leave the room.

I am always sure to thank the angel or angels that come to me even though they don't expect thanks. It's just common courtesy in my opinion. It's also my way of expressing to them how I love and appreciate their assistance. Everyone may not have the ability to sense or see the angels, but they want all of us to know they are there to help us with anything we ask for, and they are continually making slight adjustments in each of our lives day-to-day when we ask for their guidance.

Early in this book I talked about my ability to see and communicate with angels when I was a child. Although I very rarely get a glimpse of a "human-looking" angel now, I continue to have experiences that stun, astonish and humble me. I'm a believer among believers, but I am still amazed by their astounding grace.

I will be writing information about the differences between guardian angels, Archangels and spirit guides during this chapter, but first I want to talk about some of my personal experiences with these beings. I've had so many beautiful occurrences when I have asked for angel comfort or guidance and can't possibly put them all in this chapter but I want to tell you about some of my most striking incidents with them.

The following is my most common experience. It occurs when I ask for their company for any reason. After my request to hear from them, I promptly begin to see dazzling lights twinkling above and around me. When these lights appear, it often looks as if someone has thrown a handful of illuminated gold glitter into the air. This is what has replaced the ability I had as a child to see them in a physical shape. However my ability to hear and feel them has never diminished. Although I only hear occasional words, I receive their thoughts clearly and feel a tremendous energy surge when they enter a room.

I frequently hear a high pitch ringing in one of my ears. This occurs probably at least once or twice a week. When I hear this sound, know I am receiving a sort of "download" of information I will need in the near future. Usually, the ringing just lasts a few seconds to a minute. What I've noticed though is that following one of these ear ringing occurrences (usually within a day or so), something happens where facts come to me that I didn't previously know. I'm then able to help someone in need with this freshly attained information. Whether it is a friend, family member, or client, I am suddenly able to assist in a way 24 hours earlier I would have been of little help. Before the download, I had no knowledge of that particular situation or topic.

Another method angels use to communicate with me occurs during many of my sessions with clients. I will ask for the angels to take part in our conversation and many times I will call on a particular Archangel. Within seconds, I feel a tingling and warm sensation followed by goosebumps starting in my left arm and spreading over my upper body. At that point I know they are with us. I then ask my spiritual guest questions about a client's particular health or emotional situation. I don't have to say a word out loud. I will get clear thoughts and feelings that lead me to the answers for which I am looking. It's important to say at this point that the response that I get is not always the answer my client wants to hear. Before a session, I clearly explain that I will be relaying whatever messages I receive as I receive them. If a client doesn't want the truth, they are coming to the wrong person for help. My feeling is that the truth is always more helpful in the long run and allows people to prepare for whatever might be coming. The "feel good" answers they may be looking for have no long-term benefit but rather short-term joy. These answers come to me and I respect what I've been told.

Then there are the truly mind-blowing experiences that come out of the blue where I am always stunned by the power of the angels. There was one specific evening shortly after my mom passed away. Her death was entirely unexpected following knee replacement surgery in 2008 when she was just 68 years old and in excellent health. She and I were very close and missing her was of course incredibly painful. At the same time as I was mourning my mom, many other vast issues were infiltrating my family.

My mom had always been our matriarch; she was no doubt in charge, and we all knew it. She handled all of the family issues with incredible strength and determination. It didn't matter in any way that her three children were now all grown adults with their own children. If my mom thought one of us was in trouble or in some way messing up a part of our lives, she was there like magic to make sure we got our butts back on track. There was no way my mom would allow one of her children to not have a great marriage, happiness, healthy children and be financially responsible. Now with her gone it seemed to all fall to me. I was tasked with the responsibility of dealing with the family issues that seemed to have super-sized almost overnight. *And I wasn't my mom!* I didn't have what she had to handle things the way she did. And I hadn't asked for and didn't want this responsibility.

As a family, we were suddenly dealing with an addiction issue, legal matters that came along with it, mental illness accompanied by a couple of suicide attempts, two divorces, and several other difficulties, all with ONE family member (who I will not identify for privacy reasons) and all in the same year! There was a point around this same time when a serious decision had to be made about this family member. It was incredibly hard for all of us. I had the complete support of my entire family, but I knew the final decision rested on my shoulders. My dad was trying to help the best he could from 1,100 miles away, but he was still suffering from the loss of his wife of almost 50 years. Plus, he was in his early 70's at the time, and I wanted desperately to protect him from as much of the ugliness as possible. At the same time, I was trying to go about living my life as a mom, wife and business owner. I had three teenagers of my own at the time and all the drama that comes along with them. If you have or have had teenagers, you can relate to the need to protect them while dealing with their opposition and necessity to fight for their independence. This was a large part of my existence and also stressful at this same time.

On this particular night, I was missing my mom and wrestling with the decision I had made that had significant consequences for my relative. Anyone who has experienced the loss of someone they love knows the pain is constant but can randomly intensify in horrific waves. Between the loss of my mom and the stress from everything going on around me this particular night, it all became too much.

My husband was away on one of the trips he regularly flies as an airline pilot. I got into bed alone, rested my head on my pillow, took a deep breath, and suddenly everything became just too overwhelming. I let my emotions take over. I cried and cried and begged God for help. I needed a sign that I was making the right decisions for everyone. I felt so much pressure and responsibility, and I certainly didn't understand how I had become the one in charge. How did I end up with my mom's lifelong position in the family and where was she to guide me? Why with all my spiritual abilities was I not hearing her and feeling her around me? I freely admit it was no doubt indulging in an evening of feeling sorry for myself.

As I was lying on my bed sobbing, I felt a familiar energy enter my bedroom. At first I was desperately hoping it was my mom coming for a visit but within a few seconds I recognized it as the energy of an angel. I was certainly happy to welcome an angel but still this was something I had felt many times. Tonight it didn't feel like an angel coming to me was going to be enough.

The angel that arrived apparently was completely aware of the fact that at I needed more than a visit this time because, over the next 30 minutes, there was so much more to come. I felt the presence of this incredibly beautiful energy lying next to me on the bed. Within seconds, there was this intense feeling of the softest, warmest, purest hug I have ever experienced. I immediately realized that I was being wrapped in the wings of my angelic visitor. There are no words to describe how this felt. I'm doing my best, but there aren't human words that I know of to express this feeling. I was immediately comforted but not expected to stop crying or for my pain to cease. I was just being soothed and told what I was feeling was okay and that I was not going through it all alone. Falling asleep is always a challenge for me even on a good night, but shortly after the arrival of my celestial friend I was sound asleep. I woke up feeling I had an excellent night's sleep and just knew that I could handle what was in front of me. I had spent the night being held in the arms of an angel.

Many of my experiences occurred during a time in my life when I was trying to make a decision that was a bit overwhelming. I've found that the number 1111 often appears at the same time period that I happen to be double guessing a choice or decision. I know since I have seen 1111 all of my life that this is a sign the angels are with me. They are guiding me and supporting me with the decision I was facing.

As part of this chapter, I want to discuss the differences in angels, Archangels and spirit guides. The information below covers who they are, their differences and what role they each play our world.

Guardian Angels

You have at least one guardian angel that has been with you since your soul incarnated into your body and before you took your first breath. Other guardian angels come to you during certain periods in your life when you may need extra protection or guidance. It may be disappointing to learn, but the truth is angels have never been human with only a few very rare exceptions. Our dead loved ones are not angels. They CAN, however, be spirit guides and watch over, protect you and assist you in all areas of your life. But your real guardian angel will be with you when your soul transitions and will help to guide you to the other side at the time of your physical death. This angel stays with you through everything you do in your life.

Your guardian angel watches over you through your successes and helps you through all the obstacles you encounter. He or she will support you no matter what choices you make and will be there for you when you are in physical danger or when you need spiritual support. If it is not your time to die, your guardian angel will step in and save you. Your guardian angel will help you while you fulfill your life's purpose. They know the true you. They know you on a soul level even though you're now in human form. Listen for their guidance. They are there for you always and will help you, with your permission in any area of your life. Just ask for their assistance.

Archangels

Archangels are the leaders of the angels. They can be in many places at the same time. I often hear people tell me that they are afraid to bother the Archangels with their problems when there are so many people with bigger issues in the world. This is not a factor. Your concerns are as significant to the Archangels as any person on the planet. The most famous of all the Archangels are Michael, Raphael, Gabriel, and Uriel. Each of these Archangels is mentioned in the Bible many times. I discuss these four Archangels below, but there are many other Archangels; I encourage you to research and learn more about them. They each have a distinct role in our lives.

Archangel Michael's name means "Who is like God", "Like unto God", "Who is like the Divine". Michael is the first angel created by God. He is the leader of all the Archangels. He is in charge of protection, courage, and strength. Archangel Michael also oversees the lightworkers and their missions. Michael carries a sword that he uses to protect us and cut through etheric cords.

When Michael is around, you may be able to see purple or blue light. If you feel you are under spiritual attack, need direction, protection or purpose, call on Michael and he will be there. Michael is also known as the "Patron Saint of Police Officers". Michael is superb with electronics like computers, appliances and cars. He is the angel I call on most often for myself and my clients, and he has never disappointed me.

Archangel Raphael's name means "Healing power of God", "The Divine has healed", "God heals". He is a powerful healer and assists with all forms of healing whether in humans or animals. You can call upon Raphael to heal the mind, body and spirit. I ask for his assistance with clients often in my practice. Raphael will also help on behalf of someone you love if you ask. However as with all angels he cannot interfere with the free will of the other person. In other words, he cannot force treatment.

I had one particular healing session that was especially moving. As with most healing sessions, I called on Archangel Raphael for his help. I felt him enter the room as he normally does when I call. This session was an especially serious case with a client suffering from well-advanced Lyme disease that had gone undiagnosed for almost 20 years. During the healing, I felt a light touch on my left hand and then a slight pull so that my arm was a bit behind me. I did not resist this at all since I was very aware that Raphael was in charge. With my right hand still on my client, I felt a surge of energy and saw flashes of green and white light. Raphael was intensifying my energy to assist in the healing. It was one of the most incredible healing experiences I have every encountered.

Raphael is known to be one of the most cheerful of all the Archangels. As the "Patron Saint of Travelers", you can call upon him when you travel to ensure you have a safe trip. He can even make sure your bags don't get lost by the airline when you are flying. He also assists when asked to help find lost pets, personal items and with addiction cravings.

Archangel Gabriel's name means "Strength of God"; "The Divine is my strength"; "God is my strength". She is the messenger of Spirit. Gabriel delivers messages but does not interfere with a person's free will. She will simply deliver the message and stand by with the hope of supporting you in your reaction. Gabriel is known to help connect to the Universal life force and help us understand our life's path. She is also the bringer of good news and hope. In the Bible, Gabriel is said to be the angel who appeared to Mary to tell her of the impending birth of Christ. If you are considering starting a family, she is there to assist you with the conception and birth or through an adoption process. She is also the Archangel to call on when you become lost regarding your life's purpose and direction. She is very powerful and will gently push you in the right direction.

Archangel Uriel's name means "God is light", "God's light", Fire of God". Uriel is considered one of the wisest of all the Archangels. He is known as being very practical, intelligent and creative. He is also subtle in his actions. He enjoys sending someone a great new idea without the person ever knowing the idea originated from him. His areas of knowledge are divine magic, alchemy, weather and Earth changes. He assists those who are afflicted by natural disasters. Uriel links humans with the spiritual realm. Archangel Uriel shows us how to heal all aspects of our lives. He is exceptionally gifted at allowing us to acknowledge our blessings when we are having troubles in our lives. He brings unconditional forgiveness to the world.

There are many other Archangels that are here to assist us with their guidance. Don't hesitate to call on any of them when you feel the need.

Spirit Guides

Spirit guides are highly evolved souls that unlike angels once lived on the Earthly plane as human beings. When we decide to incarnate in a human body while still in the spirit world, we choose a guide that supports us from the time of birth until our physical death. Sometimes they follow us through several lives as our guide. They are sometimes people we knew in past lives, and because they know what it's like to be on Earth in human form, they are fantastic teachers for us. They understand the emotions and restrictions involved with being human. However unlike us they remember precisely what exists in the spiritual realm. Our spirit guides never leave us and will always be there when we ask for their assistance. They know our life purpose and are there when we get off our path.

delivers messages but does not interfere with a person's free will. She will simply deliver the message and stand by with the hope of supporting you in your reaction. Gabriel is known to help connect to the Universal life force and help us understand our life's path. She is also the bringer of good news and hope. In the Bible, Gabriel is said to be the angel who appeared to Mary to tell her of the impending birth of Christ. If you are considering starting a family, she is there to assist you with the conception and birth or through an adoption process. She is also the Archangel to call on when you become lost regarding your life's purpose and direction. She is very powerful and will gently push you in the right direction.

Archangel Uriel's name means "God is light", "God's light", Fire of God". Uriel is considered one of the wisest of all the Archangels. He is known as being very practical, intelligent and creative. He is also subtle in his actions. He enjoys sending someone a great new idea without the person ever knowing the idea originated from him. His areas of knowledge are divine magic, alchemy, weather and Earth changes. He assists those who are afflicted by natural disasters. Uriel links humans with the spiritual realm. Archangel Uriel shows us how to heal all aspects of our lives. He is exceptionally gifted at allowing us to acknowledge our blessings when we are having troubles in our lives. He brings unconditional forgiveness to the world.

There are many other Archangels that are here to assist us with their guidance. Don't hesitate to call on any of them when you feel the need.

Spirit Guides

Spirit guides are highly evolved souls that unlike angels once lived on the Earthly plane as human beings. When we decide to incarnate in a human body while still in the spirit world, we choose a guide that supports us from the time of birth until our physical death. Sometimes they follow us through several lives as our guide. They are sometimes people we knew in past lives, and because they know what it's like to be on Earth in human form, they are fantastic teachers for us. They understand the emotions and restrictions involved with being human. However unlike us they remember precisely what exists in the spiritual realm. Our spirit guides never leave us and will always be there when we ask for their assistance. They know our life purpose and are there when we get off our path.

leader of all the Archangels. He is in charge of protection, courage, and strength. Archangel Michael also oversees the lightworkers and their missions. Michael carries a sword that he uses to protect us and cut through etheric cords.

When Michael is around, you may be able to see purple or blue light. If you feel you are under spiritual attack, need direction, protection or purpose, call on Michael and he will be there. Michael is also known as the "Patron Saint of Police Officers". Michael is superb with electronics like computers, appliances and cars. He is the angel I call on most often for myself and my clients, and he has never disappointed me.

Archangel Raphael's name means "Healing power of God", "The Divine has healed", "God heals". He is a powerful healer and assists with all forms of healing whether in humans or animals. You can call upon Raphael to heal the mind, body and spirit. I ask for his assistance with clients often in my practice. Raphael will also help on behalf of someone you love if you ask. However as with all angels he cannot interfere with the free will of the other person. In other words, he cannot force treatment.

I had one particular healing session that was especially moving. As with most healing sessions, I called on Archangel Raphael for his help. I felt him enter the room as he normally does when I call. This session was an especially serious case with a client suffering from well-advanced Lyme disease that had gone undiagnosed for almost 20 years. During the healing, I felt a light touch on my left hand and then a slight pull so that my arm was a bit behind me. I did not resist this at all since I was very aware that Raphael was in charge. With my right hand still on my client, I felt a surge of energy and saw flashes of green and white light. Raphael was intensifying my energy to assist in the healing. It was one of the most incredible healing experiences I have every encountered.

Raphael is known to be one of the most cheerful of all the Archangels. As the "Patron Saint of Travelers", you can call upon him when you travel to ensure you have a safe trip. He can even make sure your bags don't get lost by the airline when you are flying. He also assists when asked to help find lost pets, personal items and with addiction cravings.

Archangel Gabriel's name means "Strength of God"; "The Divine is my strength"; "God is my strength". She is the messenger of Spirit. Gabriel

There are times when additional spirit guides can come into our life for a period of time to assist us through an inevitable transition or change in our lives. This is also pre-planned. Spirit guides are crucial to us as humans to lead us to the lessons we are meant to learn in this lifetime.

Many people want to know the name of their spirit guide, and that can be acquired. One way to learn your guides name is to do a meditation where you ask your spirit guide to whisper his or her name in your ear. You may hear a name, or a name will come to you as a thought.

All of these mystical, magical beings exist in the spiritual world and visit our physical world all the time. We are blessed with the assistance of angels, spirit guides, fairies, and other elementals and so much more. Whether you ever learn the name of your guide or guardian angel, whether you someday get to see a fairy, believe that they are here protecting you, protecting nature, and watching over every living aspect of your existence just waiting for the chance to be of assistance.

"Everything around us is made up of energy. To attract positive things in your life, start by giving off positive energy." ~ Unknown

Chapter 12

Everything is Energy and Energy Can Heal

As with most of the topics I've talked about throughout this book I have my own theory on many of the aspects of energy and its effectiveness in healing. My feelings come from the "just knowing" that I have trusted, believed in and lived by my entire life. I will share with you my beliefs about the creation of energy, how and why it can be used and more in this chapter.

First let's talk about the facts as we know them. Einstein proved many years ago that energy equals mass (E=MC). Everything in the universe is made up of energy. That includes your body, your furniture, the trees outside your window and even the food on your plate. Energy is the building block of all matter. It is always flowing and changing form. Energy presents itself in different shapes and forms even though it is all made up of the same thing.

There are several different types of energy. Some are more readily converted or transformed than others. For example, an easy way to convert energy is by burning wood in your fireplace. The wood that is chemical energy converts into heat and light energy. Plant transform light energy into chemical energy through the process of photosynthesis. Engines can transform chemical energy into kinetic energy, etc. Each type of energy converts differently, but energy can never die. What we learn by knowing this information is that energy can take on any form and can never cease to exist.

What we don't know though is where did energy originate? It's a difficult question to answer. Many would say that energy originated from the Sun. The sun was created by a massive cloud of gas and dust called Nebula. This ball of gas then collapsed in on itself due to the force of gravity and ignited a thermonuclear fusion. Since it's a well-known fact that energy cannot be created or destroyed only converted, it would make sense that energy existed even before the formation of the Universe. Did this energy then create the Sun?

My belief is that God was the original Creator from what all energy was formed. Whether because He manifested an event like the big bang or something else, God was the first creation made from energy. God is the Universe. God is everything. Everything is a part of God. Everything is part of His energy. We certainly can and do have many scientific, religious and metaphysical debates about this, but the truth is no one actually knows for sure. It did take place almost 5 billion years ago. So all we can have is a belief, faith, conjecture, and theories.

When we discuss healing with energy, we are doing another type of energy conversion. We have different levels of our body. They are physical, etheric, emotional, mental and astral. We are not just physically affected by illness and disease, by toxins and negativity, but the other levels of our bodies existing in and around our physical body are also affected. The physical is the only solid form of energy we see. This explains why the holistic approach to caring for ourselves has become so important in recent years. We are now fully aware of the etheric, emotional, mental and astral levels in addition to the physical. It is then logical that the levels outside of the physical body can have an effect on our wellbeing.

We talked about chakras in Chapter 5. I explained then that the chakras are energy storage centers. The emotions, traumas and events that we experienced today as well as those experienced many years ago formed patterns that are now stored in our chakras. If not dealt with, they can manifest as unbalanced energy. Unbalanced energy manifests as disease. This is where chakra healing becomes so important. However, most people don't understand why or how energy healing works because it cannot, unlike Einstein's theory, be proven. Unless you've experienced the healing power of energy yourself, it may not be easy to comprehend. Once you have experienced it, no scientist is needed to explain anything. All you know is that you are better, happier and healthier.

I would like to give you my philosophy on why I believe energy healing such as Reiki works. Remembering that everything is made out of energy, if I focus my energy on a client's chakras, I can transform their energy and raise the client's vibrational frequency to the same level as mine. As a client, you might feel warmth, peacefulness, and an overall sense of wellbeing. This is energy healing. The same is true with healing an injury or illness no matter where it has manifested in the body. The ailment is created by the dysfunctional energy centers (chakras) so by clearing and cleaning them, I am assisting in the healing process. This is in no way meant to make anyone think that energy work can replace modern medicine. I completely disagree with those that feel they have the capacity to heal a disease with no medical diagnosis, involvement or treatment. Energy healing is an incredible add-on to traditional medicine. Long before science created medicine and other treatments for illness, people still got sick, survived and got well. God gave us the ability to heal ourselves and each other by using our energy. He also gave us energy medicine in the form of crystals, herbal medicine, pressure points throughout our bodies, colors, etc. We are very blessed to live in a time when modern medicine exists and is available to us, and that should always be the first avenue you explore when you become ill.

The most logical way I explain how I can help someone with energy healing is to describe how I assist the clients that regularly come to me with issues of severe depression. They are already being treated by medical doctors and have been prescribed medicine like anti-depressants, mood stabilizers, tranquilizers, etc., however they still feel depressed and sometimes worse than before because they also now feel heavily drugged. I have never and will never recommend anyone stop their medication for any illness. Instead, I use my ability to heal with energy to remove any residue still existing in their chakras that could be blocking the drug from doing what it can and should be doing. I feel that energy work helps the medication do what's it's meant to do to its full potential. Again, we have to get to the root cause of the illnesses existence. The medication takes care of the leftover symptoms from there. This is true not just for depression and mental illnesses, but for any disease, illness or injury.

Energy medicine can and does help hundreds of thousands of people.

You don't have to understand or even believe in it for it to work. It will always do its job. Negative, yucky energy can be transformed into positive, healthy energy just like the fire burning in your fireplace transforms wood into heat and light.

There are many forms of energy healing, and additional modalities are being developed all the time. The field of energy medicine is so extensive today because of each practitioner's background, education, and natural gifts. Energy healers can be of enormous assistance to you in many health situations. There are many modalities available, and they are each effective and should be considered when you are ill, just not at your best, or you feel like you are stuck.

The science and the proof will come. I do believe it will happen. But I have successfully used modalities such as Reiki, crystals, sound therapy, vibrational therapy, reflexology, aromatherapy and others. I am always learning about new and exciting forms of the healing arts. My hope is that everyone at some point experiences the power that energy healing has to offer. Not only is it physically healing, but it heals on the unseen energy levels of our body as well. All of these make up how we function, how we feel and who we are.

"What we are today comes from our thoughts of yesterday, and our present thoughts build our life of tomorrow: Our life is the creation of our mind."
~ Buddha

Chapter 13

The Scoop on the Law of Attraction

"All that we are is the result of what we have thought." – Buddha

The Law of Attraction has existed for thousands of years. However in the last decade or two it has become a best-selling topic and the center of many conversations. The reason for its popularity has a lot to do with plain old common sense backing it up. In addition to that though is the alluring need to have some control over our lives and our futures.

There are seven universal laws of nature. They are the Law of Mentalism, the Law of Correspondence, the Law of Vibration, the Law of Polarity, the Law of Cause and Effect, the Law of Rhythm and the Law of Gender. All seven of these work in concert with each other.

You will notice that the Law of Attraction is not explicitly mentioned as one of the seven Universal Laws. This is because the Law of Attraction is the very basic law of the Universe, which goes through all seven Universal Laws. It is through the knowledge of the Law of Attraction that you can get a better understanding of each of the seven Universal Laws.

The Law of Attraction is a simple concept. What you give you receive.

You attract whatever you choose to put your attention towards whether wanted to not. In other words, the type of habitual thinking you do will draw those same kinds of thoughts and occurrences into your life including your relationships, health, and finances. So, what type of energy you put out in the Universe comes back to you.

In the last chapter, we talked about energy. Everything is energy including your thoughts, and it is all vibrating at different frequencies. The basic premise of the Law of Attraction is like attracts like. You attract to you the same vibrational response that you put out to the world. This is determined by your attitude. Your outlook on life is the most important piece in using the Law of Attraction in your life. Your attitude creates your thoughts, which creates energy. A positive attitude attracts positive experiences. A negative attitude invites negative experiences. Again behind every thought is energy. When you are angry, you send off an energy vibration of anger that will come back to you in a similar form. Energy can only transform not die. If you put out positive energy, that in turn will be the type of response you will get back.

You are part of one large Universal Mind from which all things manifest. That makes nothing separate from each of us. We are all connected. You can, therefore, affect other's vibrational energy around you. You can do this by having a more positive outlook and causing people to function at the same vibrational level as you. When you want something think about it, feel how it will feel to attain it, and that will raise your energy vibration. If however you feel that your idea or need has no hope, then you are sabotaging yourself. You will only attract negative people and circumstances into your life because you are vibrating on that level. If you are vibrating at a positive level, then you are attracting people and circumstances at that same level. People that never give up on their dreams and always believe they will eventually achieve what they desire are the people vibrating at the level that attracts good.

Obviously change is hard. When you have lived your life-limiting your potential turning that around takes work. That is not only change but actual inner work. These are two things people tend to shy away from. The Law of Attraction is always there working its magic, but the key is it always matches up with your true vibration.

People often struggle with this issue. Most of the time, we are attracting by accident and not by choice. We are just going through our day dealing with the problems that are popping up, putting out fires so to speak. We tend to feel we don't have enough of anything. We need more money, a better job, a nicer car or whatever, which in turn creates (attracts) more lack. But by forcing our attention on our problems and the things we don't have, we are in actuality creating more problems and more lack into our lives. On the other hand when we are enjoying our day and experiencing happiness, we are attracting more joy and love into our lives. This goes back to Chapter 10 where we discussed choosing to be happy.

The truth is there is a very simple way to have everything you want and need in your life by just paying attention to where you put your thoughts. If you experience something negative during your day instead of dwelling on that negative situation, focus your attention on something positive. For example your monthly electric bill arrives, and it is $75 more than what you expected. That might cause you to become upset and start thinking thoughts that are negative. You might think; "How am I going to pay this?"; "What happened that caused this bill to be so high?"; or you might place blame and feel angry towards a friend or family member that you believe may have helped cause the increase. You may even blame the electric company itself. So what do you do? Nothing is going to make that bill become magically $75 less. Well, what you don't want to do is allow the higher bill to bring you to a place where negative thought patterns begin. Instead turn your focus to something that you want that makes you feel good. In the example of the electric bill, you take a breath, accept that the situation is what it is, and the bill amount is what it is, and take care of it without putting too much vibrational energy into it. This could mean having to make a payment arrangement with the electric company, borrowing money from a friend or relative, or not buying something else that you planned on buying this month. The point is not to put your focus on the negative feelings that came along with the higher electric bill. Instead solve the problem quickly and put your attention towards something you want that is positive. Focus your attention strongly on what specifically it is that you desire, and this attention alone will raise your energy vibration. Allow your energy to vibrate at that high frequency for as long as possible. Feel what it feels like to already have what you want. Smell it, taste it and experience it. Then it's just a matter of sitting back and allowing what you want to come to you.

Always be sure to let go of any type of resistance you may feel and believe that whatever it is that you want will come to you because of the mere fact that you want it.

"Think about any attachments that are depleting your emotional reserves. Consider letting them go".
~ Oprah Winfrey

Chapter 14

Those Pesky Little Etheric Cords

I would imagine you are already wondering what is an etheric cord? Let's start with a description. An etheric cord is an energetic connection that forms between two people.

During the course of your day, you are most likely in contact with many people either in person, via telephone or email. When you are in touch with a person frequently, an etheric (energy) cord forms where energy is regularly exchanged. Each person is sending and receiving energy at different vibrations. When you feel love towards a person, you develop an even stronger etheric cord. These cords form between the people you are closest to like your spouse, children, parents, and siblings. However cords also regularly form between friends, co-workers and others.

When I describe what these cords look like to a client, I explain they resemble a type of clear tubing. This tubing can connect between you and another person at any of the chakra points. These cords form naturally and exchange energy between you and the person on the other end. You may notice the cords existing in a way that seems like a coincidence. A typical example of this would be when you are thinking of someone, say your sister, and maybe wondering how she is doing. Suddenly the phone rings. Guess who is on the other end? Your sister! This often happens because once a cord exists between you and another person, energy then travels through the etheric cord between the two of you and causes exchanges of thoughts and feelings.

When a relationship is created from a fear-based emotion such as loneliness, anger, co-dependency, abuse, addiction, lack of forgiveness or other damaging emotions the cords often turn negative.

This is especially true after break-ups, divorces, and other life changing events. Once the relationship has become cynical or after it ends, the etheric cord still exists. The energy traveling to and from you through the cord is now negative and draining even though you may no longer be in contact with the person attached to the other end. That person is still connected to you energetically and emotionally and in some situations they are still using your energy for survival. Maybe they don't want the relationship to be over, and because they are stuck, they think about you throughout much of their day. The feelings they are experiencing can vary many times throughout a day. One moment they may miss you and feel sad, the next they may be reminiscing about good times then within a moment they may feel angry.

Once an etheric cord becomes negative, it must be dealt with through an etheric cord severing. You will know the cord has become negative if it is preventing you from moving on in your life. Sometimes it feels impossible to let go of the relationship. You may find your mind wandering to that other person without any reason because at that very same moment they are thinking about you which then initiates the energy exchange. An etheric cord severing can be very helpful to rebalance your energy and to release the cord permanently. This severing treatment will release dysfunctional aspects of the past relationship and allow you to move forward, forgive and let go.

An important question people often ask is if they sever the cord does it mean the relationship is over for good and that there will be no more feelings between you. That may not be what you want if the cord is between you and your child, parent or someone else you wish to preserve in your life. Severing the cord does not mean that the relationship has to end. Instead, the removal of the cord will allow a loving form of energy to grow between you. Whether you continue to have the person in your life or not once the cord is cut, healthy energy forms and seals the cord at the chakra level allowing your energy center to heal.

You can go to a spiritual practitioner who can professionally perform an etheric cord severing or you can sever the cords on your own. To do this requires simple focus, visualization, relaxation and calling in Archangel Michael.

To sever an etheric cord or to sever all of the etheric cords attached to you, first find a quiet spot where you can be alone. Close your eyes and take a deep breath in through your nose allowing your belly to fill with air and then slowly exhaling through your mouth. Do this three times. Once you completed the breaths, you should feel relaxed. Now either out loud or in your mind request Archangel Michael to come to you. Within a couple of moments, you should feel his warm, peaceful and comforting presence. Once you feel Archangel Michael's company say the following:

"Archangel Michael, I ask you to sever any etheric cords that are attached to my body that are negative and harmful to my well-being and highest good."

When you perform this exercise with your eyes closed, you may be able to see the cords being cut, see intense colors (especially violet) or feel the cords releasing and detaching from various chakras. After this exercise is completed, you should feel a calm peacefulness come over you, and you may even feel lighter. If you feel it is necessary, repeat this cleansing as often as needed. When you have people in your lives that are draining energy but are still essential in your life, you may need to practice this daily. Healers, caregivers, therapists, empaths and anyone who is nurturing can develop etheric cords that drain them. They can suffer from many illnesses like chronic fatigue, depression, and anxiety.

The etheric cords that attach between people and become negative must be severed for each of our health and overall wellbeing. You can find several meditations online if you are interested in doing this on your own or find a professional practitioner to assist you in the process. Your life will be improved dramatically once these cords are released.

"Of course you don't die. Nobody dies. Death doesn't exist. You only reach a new level of vision, a new realm of consciousness, a new unknown world." ~ Henry Miller

Chapter 15

There is No Death

"You don't have a soul. You are a soul. You have a body." – C.S. Lewis

This is a very important chapter to me. Much of my "just knowing" comes from my memories of a magnificent spiritual world. I desperately want everyone to feel as I do and not fear death. There very simply is no true death so there is nothing to fear.

I've talked a lot about energy throughout the last pages. I've explained that our bodies are energy and so are our souls. As I've stated multiple times, energy cannot and does not die, but only transforms. That is true at the time of the physical death of our bodies.

I have memories of the spiritual world. I have had these memories my entire life. I remember being able to think of a place or a person I wanted to be near and manifest it right there on the spot. Simply with my thought came my desire. I remember specifically enjoying a grassy spot with a beautiful waterfall surrounded by wildflowers. Usually, I liked to visit this place alone to rest and rejuvenate. Oh, I remember the colors so clearly! The colors of the flowers, the grass, the water and everything else around me are impossible to describe. We don't have colors like that in our world. Anytime I wanted to be with someone I loved I just thought of them, and they appeared. Not as a vision but as a being I could converse with and share loving memories. I remember this particular place being my favorite spot. It was like a secret area I had created just for me. I don't remember every detail of this other world and I'm sure that's by design, but I am lucky enough to have been permitted to retain some of my memories, and I hope the reason for that is so I can pass it on to others to bring them comfort.

THE MOMENT OF DEATH

The moment of death is called a "moment" because technically you are either alive, or you are dead. However, many people who have had near-death experiences explain it as a process that lasted much longer than a moment. When your body is clinically dead, your heart stops beating, and blood stops circulating which means blood no longer flows to your brain. Within about 10 seconds all brain activity stops. Interestingly people who have had near-death experiences recall situations that occurred after the brain had stopped functioning.

In 1907, a doctor named Duncan MacDougall, from Haverhill, Massachusetts created an experiment to attempt to weigh the soul. When a patient was in the process of dying they were placed on scales that were very sensitive. At the exact time of death, the body would lose approximately ¾ of an ounce. With absolutely no logical reason for this, Dr. MacDougall concluded that the ¾ of an ounce must be the weight of the soul leaving the body. To my knowledge, the weight loss at the moment of death remains unchallenged although of course there are other theories as to its precise cause. Now we are circling back to the fact that energy never dies. But also remember that energy cannot exist without matter of some form. This must mean that the soul takes the electrical energy of the body with it when it leaves its host. There is a theory now that particles of the soul may contain neutrinos, which pass through all other types of matter. This would explain the ability for souls to travel anywhere with ease.

Your body is simply that, your body. Your soul resides in your body for this lifetime. When you die, your soul is not limited or confined by the human body. Instead, your soul energy is released, and you become a vibrating ball of energy. In this state, you are able to begin the process of visiting places and people in a flash. There are many stories I have heard and probably you have as well of people who were visited by someone they thought was a living relative within seconds or minutes of that person's death. Shortly after this spiritual visit, they were told that the loved one had passed away around that same time.

Sometimes the soul can be confused or even shocked at the moment of death. This is especially true if it has been a tragic and sudden death or a situation where a suicide has occurred. Even though you choose your time of death before incarnating, there can still be much confusion when it is sudden. In cases like this the soul can choose to linger on Earth for a period of time until they understand what has happened and then they are free to move on.

I remember being with my mom in the Intensive Care Unit of the hospital where she had arrived ten days earlier to have knee replacement surgery. She developed a condition called ARDS (Acute Respiratory Distress Syndrome) while in the hospital. We were all called to Florida by my dad when he was told she was "not going to make it." I sat in her ICU room day after day with my family and watched my mom dying. Of course, I wasn't accepting that she was going to die at this point. I was fighting it and telling the doctors they were not permitted to give her a death sentence when there is always hope and the possibility of a miracle. I spent much of my time with her talking to her about good memories and using my skills as a Reiki Master in an attempt to heal her. I would pray and ask for angels to come into the room to help make her well. In hindsight, I know the angels were there, but I think it was more for comfort than for the healing of my mom.

About the third day I was there, I remember distinctly looking at my mom and feeling her soul was gone from her body. Later that same day I felt it had returned and that she was back in her body. Over the next few days, I felt her soul come and go several times before her death. I believe that even though I was not ready or willing to accept what was happening at the time, I was watching my mom transition to the other side. I felt her coming and going preparing for her death. I felt that she was beginning to reunite with her parents, brother, friends and loved ones from her life. I think this may happen with many chronically ill people. In these cases, there is no shock or trauma because they are prepared at the moment of their death.

I also believe strongly that anytime there is a violent act against a person that is destined to end with their physical death, the soul has the option to leave the body before the horrific event happens. I especially believe this is true regarding children. I do not believe the souls of these victims are in their bodies when they are being brutally hurt or tortured in any way. Anyone that has lost someone tragically or violently should find comfort in this. Your loved one did not experience the last few moments of their life in their physical body in these cases. They might have chosen to watch from outside of their body if they needed to experience what was happening or instead they may have decided to move on, so they didn't have to witness the very end. My mom was given the opportunity to come and go to prepare herself and maybe her family for several days before her physical death.

When your physical body dies, your guardian angel and spirit guides will be there waiting for you. They help to transport you to the other side. This can take seconds, hours or longer depending on the soul itself. Some souls feel the need to stick around for a while to be there to help console their loved ones. This is common. It's said that many souls stay through their funerals. If there is a strong physical connection to someone, say a parent leaves young children when their body dies they may feel the need to stay longer.

LEARNING TO LIVE AGAIN AS A SOUL

So, your physical body is gone, and you are in soul form. What can you do? What do you do? What happens? You are instantly reunited with loved ones that passed before you. If someone you love has reincarnated, they often leave a piece of their energy behind in the spirit world, so you are able to have those reunions. Any negativity, anger or pain you have been holding on to is released. This sometimes takes time. There are places of rejuvenation on the other side where your soul can go to recover from its Earthly incarnation. When you have fully recovered, you are free now to review your time on Earth. This is called a "life review." You watch a sort of movie of your life and evaluate what it is that you have learned. Did you complete the tasks you were meant to complete? Did you learn the lessons you were sent to learn? This is reviewed with your guides present, and you are given time to make determinations on whether or not your soul developed in that life.

Earth time is much different than spirit time. When we are in spirit form, what feels like minutes may in actuality be years on Earth. This can be why you may get contact from a loved one who passes immediately following their death and then not again for years. To their soul, it's been just the blink of an eye. You are free to make decisions about your future. You can choose to remain in the spirit world indefinitely. You may elect to begin preparing for your next incarnation. You may want to work as a spirit guide to help people on Earth. You have many options. Many souls choose to take their time and enjoy their afterlife for a while. You may need time to reflect on what your lives have taught you. You may elect to visit other star systems. And there is no doubt during this stage you are doing some studying. You are learning about the restrictions, temptations and traumas that come with living as a human being and how you might use this information in future lives if you choose one. You may study to be a healer or spiritual teacher of some kind. There are countless amounts of subjects in which you may want to study. Most souls do a lot of visiting with loved ones and working in their spiritual groups on their soul's development.

WHERE IS HEAVEN?

While it's true that we can't find Heaven on "Google Earth" or "MapQuest" there is no doubt it does exist. The spirit world or spiritual plane is inhabited by spirits. Those who practice Christianity call this place "Heaven." Heaven is known to be where our souls reside with God, saints, angels and the ascended masters. All spirits whether good or bad are taken to this place. This place is home to all souls. We all return there upon our physical death. Of course, this does not exactly measure up with the Bible scriptures that talk about hell, however, it always has and continues now to resonate with me. I believe the souls that did well on Earth are rewarded and permitted peace, happiness and given unlimited choices in their future decisions. The souls that did evil or harm to others while on Earth are not cast into a fiery pit called "Hell." Instead, they are sent to work on making up for the damage they caused during their lifetime. They have much work to do before they are ever permitted to return to Earth again in human form.

The location of heaven or the spiritual plane may never be to us in our current form of existence, but we can certainly say it is where God exists. Because the beings that live in Heaven are always within our reach, it is difficult for me to think of them in a place that far away from us. It seems to me that it is simply another dimension of where we are now.

The Bible tends to focus on the purpose of Heaven more than its location. It may be that the location of Heaven is supposed to stay a mystery. There is nothing wrong with keeping that secret. We don't need to know physically where it is as long as we know those who reside there are within hearing distance and can come to us anytime we need their guidance, love or support.

I would like to tell you a remarkable story that occurred after my mom had been gone for a little over two months. I was reading a book on communicating with spirits. This would have been a book I would have chosen to read regardless, however with my mom's passing and my not having any communication with her since, made it definitely a more desired topic than normal even for me. I was at a section of the book where it explained that an easy way to connect with spirits was through the use of electronics like lights. They could use that physical energy to manifest more easily. I was sitting against the pillows on my bed with the light that sits on my nightstand turned on next to me. When I reached this section in the book, I asked my mom to please make the light bulb flicker to let me know she was there. After about 20 minutes of asking for this acknowledgment from her repeatedly, nothing happened. I was frustrated. I closed the book, stood up and told my mom out loud that it was obvious to me that she wasn't strong enough to flicker the light maybe because she hadn't been on the other side long enough to learn how to manipulate energy. (I admit I might have been trying to get her a little riled up.) I shut the light off and went downstairs to my office to get some work done. Without thinking about it, I walked upstairs a couple of hours later and switched the light back on. At that very second the light bulb turned on, flickered and blew out completely with a loud pop. It was not a typical light bulb burn out that we all experience commonly. It made my heart jump. I noticed my clock and other things connected to that outlet had also stopped working. I immediately fell against the wall next to me for support in utter amazement. I knew it was my mom who had created this situation. As I looked around, other things in the room also had no power. My home was only around a year old and newly built at this point. So new in fact that I didn't even know where the fuse box was located. I headed for the basement and found the electrical box and quickly discovered that the fuse to our room had completely blown. Since my husband wasn't home, I called my dad puzzled. I didn't understand how a low wattage light bulb burning out could blow a fuse. I explained the set of circumstances that began with an attempt to contact my mom to my dad. My dad told me that was highly unlikely that turning on a little lamp in a house particularly as new as ours would cause this. After talking to him for a few minutes, I had zero doubt that my mom was telling me very clearly not to question how much power she had! That was my mom's personality exactly and something she would have done to prove a point. That same circumstance has never happened again with any outlet in our house. It's been almost five years since that occurrence.

REINCARNATION

I'm finding more and more people regardless of their religion or upbringing are now becoming believers in reincarnation. Just 20 or so years ago most Christians thought it was crazy to believe in reincarnation. As of the last poll I know of which was completed sometime in the early 2000's, somewhere around 38% of the world now believes in this experience.

So where's the proof? Dr. Ian Stevenson collected the best known and well-respected research I'm aware of on this subject. There have been many scientists and doctors who have performed experiments on patients who were taken through hypnosis to either a previous life or to the spirit world while in a trance state. However, Dr. Stevenson collected thousands of cases specifically of children who without being hypnotized were able to remember past lives. He was able to use this method with much accuracy because considerable pieces of the information he received from the children was recent enough to investigate. His research was extraordinary. Dr. Stevenson, who died in 2007, documented each child's statements from a previous life. He then identified who the deceased person was from the memories of the children. When he was given the name of the deceased individual, he could then verify that the child's memories matched the facts involved. He has even been able to match birthmarks and birth defects to a wound or scar. For example, if a child recalled their previous life ending because of a bullet wound to the chest during a war, he would sometimes find a birthmark in that exact location on their new body. The facts could easily enough be verified through the decedent's medical records. Naturally, this ruled out the possibility of coincidence or a situation where a child's imagination could have been thought of as the cause of the phenomena.

Overall, Dr. Stevenson completed more than 3,000 cases. Even skeptics agree that it is the best evidence we have yet to prove reincarnation is genuine. Dr. Stevenson was a medical doctor who had many papers published before he began his work with paranormal research. You can find details on Dr. Stevenson's work by doing an internet search on his name and reading the many articles, books and pages of information that mention his astounding cases.

Reincarnation is one of the very few metaphysical or paranormal subjects of research with meticulous proof to back it up. I find this fascinating. One of the reasons I chose the field of Metaphysical Science is because I knew much of what I believed would be very difficult, if not impossible to prove. That was an irresistible challenge to me. Reincarnation may be the most amazing spiritual phenomenon with actual evidence to date.

As long as you have life and breath, believe. Believe for those who cannot. Believe even if you have stopped believing. Believe for the sake of the dead, for love, to keep your heart beating, believe. Never give up, never despair, let no mystery confound you into the conclusion that mystery cannot be yours".
- Mark Helprin, A Soldier of the Great War

Chapter 16

Why Not Just Believe?

"And above all, watch with glittering eyes the whole world around you because the greatest secrets are always hidden in the most unlikely places. Those who don't believe in magic will never find it." – Roald Dahl

Our daily lives are sometimes joyous but can be equally challenging. There are many struggles, hard lessons to be learned, pain, loss, and sorrow. But there is also beauty, joy, happiness, miracles, and endless amounts of love. I have been blessed with knowing what most can't imagine. And through me and my work I am letting others know that there is so much more out there and so much more to come for all of us after this physical life ends. There is an afterlife; a Heaven. There is a God. God has a plan for each of us and for the collective "us" as a whole that we can't possibly understand. He has boundless love for each and every one of us. He has provided the opportunity to see this truth through the eyes and words of a few.

We have become so very analytical in our thinking that if we can't see it, touch it or smell it; it must not exist. The truth is a thin veil separates our world from the world where our loved ones who have passed on, angels, spirit guides, Ascended Masters and God reside. I'm not special. You can get through that veil too. We all have the innate ability to get in touch with our psychic side and learn what I and many others already have. It's possible for you to "just know" too.

I have written this book because I am one of the few that "just know". I have been permitted to remember things that most have forgotten. I have experienced things that most will never encounter while on this planet. The only thing asked of me in return is to share these phenomenal events, memories and encounters with as many people as I possibly can to provide others with the comfort and security that comes with this gift.

Now, I leave it in your hands. You have the option to believe or not believe in what I've shared with you throughout this book. What you yourself may already instinctively "just know". If you need to find out first-hand, then you are capable of it. You need to open yourself to a part of you that has been closed down during this lifetime so far.

My final thought for this book must be this: why not just believe? Why is it that the idea of an existence outside of this world seems so unbelievable to so many? This other place has no pain, no illness and no suffering. Instead, there is only unconditional love and splendor. Why is it so easy to believe in the existence of evil, demons, Hell and conspiracies, but not believe that there can be the complete opposite? Why don't we naturally believe in a wondrous continuance of our souls' survival? Isn't the definition of faith, believing without actual proof? If you have the ability to acknowledge all of the bad and negative aspects of the world, why not recognize that there are even more aspects that are good? Why not accept all the miracles that endlessly take place around us?

I have to tell you, it feels much better to believe in the good. Won't every remaining moment of your life be so much more fantastic knowing that you are a part of something so big and amazing? So spectacular that our human minds can't even comprehend it so we have to block the memories of what that world is like just to function here and now? I think so. I know so. I believe.

We talk about faith in God, in Jesus, in whatever higher power we choose to believe in, but why put a limit on what we believe? Why not believe that angels are here right now helping us? Believe that right now, at this very moment, an angel is whispering in the ear of a small child who will someday grow up to be a healer and to teach about a world she was given the gift of learning about at a very young age. Why not just believe in magic, fairies, spirit guides, angels, psychics, the power of forgiveness and alternative ways to heal ourselves with energy?

I often ask myself why I was selected to receive this information and I honestly have never found the answer to that question. I have an awareness of many things that are beyond the physical plane of existence that are just part of what I know. I don't feel more qualified or entitled to have been given this knowledge. But I do know that I can no longer keep it to myself because of fear of what others might think. I began honoring my life purpose by studying metaphysics. Over time, I became more and more comfortable and confident as I worked with clients and realized that I was really helping them. I am not hiding this side of me anymore. I feel honored and blessed and want to tell anyone who wants to listen that there is no reason to not believe in what I've described. No reason not to have faith. Without faith, we are lost and searching for answers to questions we will never find answers to while on this planet.

I think we all see a little something more than just the physical if we are honest with ourselves. It makes no sense that the miracles happening around us are a coincidence. Whether it's the creation and subsequent birth of a baby, the meeting of soulmates, the beauty of a sunset, the vastness of an ocean, the unexplainable occurrences we label as "déjà vu", the everyday six-sense we all possess, or one of so many other unexplained phenomena, miracles are everywhere.

I know how I feel about the unseen world I wrote this book about and the beliefs I have lived my life respecting and trusting. I just believe.

"Everything happens for a reason.

Just believe!"

www.ingramcontent.com/pod-product-compliance
Lightning Source LLC
Chambersburg PA
CBHW061948070426
42450CB00007BA/1088